W9-BEM-772

The publisher gratefully acknowledges the generous contribution to this book provided by the following organizations and individuals:

ELIZABETH DUREIN

DAVID B. GOLD FOUNDATION

MOORE FAMILY FOUNDATION

and by the General Endowment Fund of the Associates of the University of California Press.

The Intertidal Wilderness

THE INTERTIDAL WILDERNESS

A Photographic Journey through Pacific Coast Tidepools

Anne Wertheim Rosenfeld

Revised Edition   *With Robert T. Paine*

UNIVERSITY OF CALIFORNIA PRESS   *Berkeley   Los Angeles   London*

University of California Press
Berkeley and Los Angeles, California

University of California Press, Ltd.
London, England

Library of Congress Cataloging-in-Publication Data

Rosenfeld, Anne Wertheim, 1951–
    The intertidal wilderness : a photographic journey
through Pacific Coast tidepools / Anne Wertheim
Rosenfeld with Robert T. Paine.—Rev. ed.
        p.   cm.
Includes bibliographical references (p.   ) and index.
    ISBN 0-520-23193-7 (cloth : alk. paper)—
    ISBN 0-520-21705-5 (pbk. : alk. paper)
    1.   Intertidal ecology—Pacific Coast (North America).
2.   Intertidal ecology.   I.   Paine, Robert T., 1933– .
II.   Title.

QH95.3.R67   2002
577.69'9—dc21   2001001833

Manufactured in Korea

11   10   09   08   07   06   05   04   03   02
10   9   8   7   6   5   4   3   2   1

The paper used in this publication meets the minimum
requirements of ANSI/NISO Z39.48-1992 (R 1997)
(*Permanence of Paper*).⊗

To Matthew A. Rosenfeld

Contents

Preface *Robert T. Paine*

Seventeen years have elapsed since our initial attempt to meld the photographically captured and sometimes violent beauty of rocky intertidal shores with an interpretive text focused on the ecological processes underlying their patterns. These shores experience unique physical stresses, in the form of heavy wave action and desiccating low tides; furthermore, the resident organisms often interact with an intensity difficult to imagine from an entirely terrestrial perspective. Our goal, both originally and now, therefore, is to guide the eye to telltale signs of ecological relationships, to permit the seashore explorer to interpret the natural history of the resident species. For only with understanding comes respect.

How has the book been modified, extended, and improved? For one thing, we have rearranged old and added new photographs, and updated the scientific references. We have also added a chapter, "Nature's Variability: Understanding the Changing Patterns, Conserving the Species," which focuses on the effects of anthropogenic change on rocky shores: pollution, overfishing, introduction of exotic species, global warming. Recognizing and confronting such issues is becoming increasingly urgent, for the last seventeen years have not been kind to most seashores and their biological assemblages. Our understanding of ecological processes has also increased in the intervening years, and the current book attempts to capture these as well. For instance, the notion of a "trophic cascade," in which benefits accrue to other species not directly involved in a chain of relationships—sea otters eating sea urchins, thus benefiting the marine algae that urchins prey on, for example—are commonplace on rocky shores and often involve species whose ecological roles are subtle. These bit players, however, contribute substantially to the system's biodiversity, and the biology involved is often spectacular. Yet can the purposeful preservation of, say, sea anemones and their allies, bryozoa, sponges, nudibranchs, or even intertidal fishes, be justified by scientific arguments? Or will an esthetically based appeal remain the most convincing defense for the myriad species populating rocky shores, adding beauty and interest, but whose ecological contribution is unknown?

Our intended audience includes both the casual seashore visitor and the dedicated enthusiast. The initial chapter introduces some major features of temperate-zone rocky shores exposed to heavy wave action. The next two chapters, "Competition" and "Predation," focus on processes that produce pattern. The fourth chapter explores reproduction and its sundry modes. The role of color is developed in Chapter 5. It is here, perhaps more than elsewhere, where the intrinsic grandeur of many intertidal plants and animals can be enjoyed without the encumbrance of scientific interpretation. Simply put, many of the dazzling hues visible on rocky shores defy logic and current understanding. The final chapter, "Nature's Variability," addresses the following quandary: if nature is dynamic and forever in flux, how can we identify and alleviate the stresses added by humanity?

We live in and contribute to a rapidly changing natural world. This book aims to encourage people of all ages to explore, appreciate, and begin to understand the biological complexity and beauty of rocky shores, and to do so as unobtrusively as possible.

Acknowledgments

I remain forever grateful to the group of people who helped make the first edition of *The Intertidal Wilderness* possible.

The development and completion of the field work and photography for this revision were assisted by the kindness and talents of a number of people, in particular Bill Dietrich and Ryan Baldwin. Thank you.

I would like to thank Norbert Wu for graciously and generously granting the use of Plate 113. My special thanks go to Laura Shapiro for her friendship and invaluable help with this project. With sadness, I thank the late Ann O'Hanlon for sharing a way of seeing that I will always cherish.

Lastly, with profound recognition for their forbearance and varied contributions, I would like to thank my husband, Bob, and my son, Matthew, for their love and support and for enduring an inflexible and disruptive tide schedule.

Anne Wertheim Rosenfeld

The revision of this book has benefited immensely from the wisdom and support of a generous and deeply committed group to whom I am particularly grateful: Mary O'Connor, Marjorie Wonham, and Chris Harley. I acknowledge with gratitude permission from the Makah Tribal Council to both observe and manipulate marine plants and animals in the Cape Flattery region, Washington State, and especially on Tatoosh Island. Generous support for the research, initiated in 1962, has come from the National Science and Mellon Foundations.

Robert T. Paine

1

Introduction

As long as there has been ocean there has been an intertidal zone. An intertidal zone, by definition the narrow belt lying between the highest and lowest tidemarks, is an "edge" that marks the interface between two very different realms: land and sea. Like many other biological edges, it can be extremely rich. One finds there not only an astounding variety of plants and animals, but also images in color, form, and texture woven layer upon layer. At the more exposed, wave-swept rocky shores along the outer coast, such as those that are the subject of this book, the landscape is hazardous but also more vivid and more varied than those shores in protected areas.

Tidal waters recede, usually twice daily, to reveal this landscape and the myriad organisms living there. During low tide one can venture out onto this terrain and wander within the seemingly providential pause in the ocean's surge. Soon the tidal waters return, modifying or rearranging the exquisite detail of this drama and refreshing the participants. Each new tide reasserts the contrast between the cosmic proportions of tidal events and the finer organic details.

The Pacific coast of North America offers one of the richest intertidal habitats in the temperate zone, north or south. Several factors contribute to this cornucopia: the upwelling of nutrient-rich bottom waters just offshore, which fertilize both the plankton and bottom-dwelling plants; a freedom from ice that elsewhere abrades the shore, and from prolonged freezes, which can wipe out resident plants and animals; frequent coastal fogs in the summertime, which protect the shore from the sun's heat; and the near absence, for reasons that continue to mystify ecologists, of herbivorous fishes.

This book focuses on the west coast of North America, where many of the common species are ubiquitous and extend from northern Baja California to the limits of the Gulf of Alaska. Even minimal familiarity with the intertidal plants and especially the animals allows one to feel at home throughout this great latitudinal range. The intertidal zone is replete with striking patterns and subtle, seemingly endless variations on some common themes. An understanding of the underlying causal processes and their visual hallmarks permits interpretation of many of these patterns. This book presents some of these patterns and, where possible, illustrates the dynamic processes that generate them.

Throughout this book, we refer to the ecological properties of populations or ensembles of populations in terms of distribution, abundance, or diversity. For marine intertidal organisms the term *distribution* contains three primary dimensions: the range of a species over geographic space, especially in the sense of physical harshness or barriers that determine latitudinal or longitudinal limits; the bathymetric range—that is, how far above and below the zero-tide datum a particular species may be found; and the fine details of an individual's immediate spatial position, including microenvironments in which only certain species are found. *Abundance* is simply an expression of whether a species is common or rare. When quantified, abundance is expressed as number of individuals per square meter, the percentage of an area occupied by some particular population, or its live weight (biomass) per unit area. *Diversity* or *biodiversity*, an ecological measure that can be either qualitative or quantitative, reflects the numbers of species inhabiting the same environment and therefore potentially interacting. Some measures can incorporate the relative abundance of the various species present as well.

The resident organisms are not haphazardly distributed along the shore but rather are arranged in distinct bands, or zones, parallel to it. The rhythm of the tides suggests that the higher zones must be occupied by organisms more resistant to the prolonged absence of water. Scientists have discovered a variety of factors governing the distribution and zonation of intertidal organisms: the strength of waves (or, conversely, the degree of shelter from the surf); the nature of the surface on which the organisms can grow (rock, cobble, or sand, and if rock, its textural qualities and degree of hardness); and the relative proportion of time spent exposed to water or air. As marine biology has evolved as a science, biologists have continued to check their ideas on distribution through experiments, and they have increasingly turned their attention to how the different animals and plants on the seashore interact, restricting or enhancing one another's distributions.

In order to describe ecological patterns, we need a system for the classification of the plants and animals involved. All known organisms have formal, scientific names, which reflect how closely related different species are and, with some added information, their evolutionary ancestry. With just a little experience, it is possible to make specific identifications.

All multicelled organisms are widely believed to have evolved from primordial cells in ancient times and seas. The animals are classified into main groups, called phyla, and the plants into divisions, according to similarities and differences that reflect evolutionary and structural relationships, not superficial appearances. Basic elements of body design, such as type of symmetry, organization of cells and tissue layers from which the body is formed, organ system development, and similarities in embryo structure, can all be important in classifying animals. Plant taxonomy is partly based on the presence of specific pigments, some of which mask the presence of others. For a more detailed description of phylogenetic relationships, see Appendix B. The classification of two common seashore animals is shown here.

	California mussel	*Giant green sea anemone*
kingdom	Animalia	Animalia
phylum	Mollusca	Cnidaria
class	Bivalvia	Anthozoa
order	Mytiloidea	Actinaria
family	Mytilidae	Actiniidae
genus	*Mytilus*	*Anthopleura*
species	californianus	xanthogrammica

3

Although common names have been created for some organisms, they often prove more confusing and cumbersome than the established scientific ones. In the Latin binomial system used in this book, the name *Mytilus californianus* is the most exact identification that can be given. Species are groups of actually or potentially interbreeding populations; yet as with individuals in the genus and species to which humanity belongs, *Homo sapiens,* members can vary considerably in behavior, appearance, or ecology. Sometimes the species to which an organism belongs is unclear. In such cases, the organism will be identified by its generic name only, followed by the abbreviation for species, "sp."

Plate 1   Wave-swept rocky shore

Plate 1 shows the rocky outer coast at the northwest tip of Washington State. One of the unusual features of the west coast of North America is that for enormous geographic stretches the outer coast is primarily composed of solid rock. Thus, the larvae of rocky shore organisms find a large target on which to settle. In contrast, the east coast of North America, especially south of Cape Cod, is predominantly sandy, and the spatially limited rocky habitat is relatively poor in species. Although many of the photographs in this book were taken in Washington State, others are from California and Alaska; taken together, they represent the suite of conspicuous plants and animals whose geographic range embraces thousands of kilometers of Pacific coast.

Plate 2   High tide

Plate 3   Low tide

Plates 2 and 3 are of an intertidal zone at both high and low tide. Along the Pacific coast of North America, four tides occur per day—two highs and two lows, each usually of different amplitude. Simply speaking, tides are a result of gravitational pulls of the sun and the moon on the earth's oceans (see Appendix A for information on tide tables). *Intertidal zone* is a general address, and all the organisms that live there share certain processes and problems attendant to staying alive. One could specify a more precise address, for in fact the intertidal zone is a conglomeration of innumerable habitats, including nooks, crannies, crevices, rock walls, surge channels, and tidepools, each with subtly different features that make them all different as places to live.

4

Plate 1

Plate 2

Plate 3

P l a t e 4   Wave action

The ocean's surge is an integral part of the daily lives of intertidal organisms.
All these organisms require water and waves to keep them moist, supply
oxygen, bring food, and remove wastes. But while they are dependent upon
the ocean, many eventually succumb to it: mussels may die from being swept
away, and other organisms may be buried in water-borne sediment.

The formidable forces of moving and breaking water can pose substantial
challenges and hazards to intertidal organisms. Biological adaptations to
minimize the risks of life in wave-swept conditions pervade the design
features of many species. Shell shape, body size, and the relative flexibility
of the stalks and stems of attached plants and animals, for instance, are all
related to contending with the stresses imposed by waves.

Where strong wave action occurs on exposed shores, one generally finds
a much broader, lusher intertidal area than in a calm, protected area with
an equivalent tidal displacement. By throwing and splashing water higher
than it would go as a result of tidal movement alone, wave action increases
the amount of rock surface that is habitable for intertidal life. Thus, on very
exposed shores, the upper limit to marine life can be 3 to 10 meters (approximately 10 to 30 feet) above the predicted tidal limits. In contrast, in those
protected habitats where the water creeps in and out with barely a ripple, tidal
amplitude, not waves, govern this boundary.

Plate 4

Plate 5   Coastal fog

Wind, waves, and fog are the hallmarks of many exposed shores. Fog forms
over the ocean when a layer of warmer air is cooled from below by the ocean.
Sometimes the sea fog sits as a stationary bank, sometimes as gossamer
filaments or streamers that appear and disappear. At other times it can roll
shoreward, cold and chilling, often associated with "fog winds" of 15–25 knots.
Although dreaded by mariners, fog is a benefit to most intertidal organisms.
It counters the relentless and often fatal baking characteristic of summertime
cloudless days and provides moisture to parched high intertidal species, many
of which can rehydrate themselves from the atmosphere in the same fashion
that household salt tends to liquefy in moist air. The mitigating effects of fog
are especially important when the timing of low water coincides with a sunny
day's maximum temperature.

8

Plate 5

Plate 6   Intertidal zonation

On rocky shores, the resident species are not haphazardly distributed on the rocks but tend to be arranged in parallel bands, or zones. Historically, it was this simple observation that attracted pioneer marine biologists to intertidal habitats. This type of biological zonation occurs when species are differentially able to survive at particular places along an environmental gradient. For example, different corals and fish inhabit different depths on a coral reef, and different trees and birds live at different elevations on a mountainside. Compared to other habitats, intertidal zonation is very compact and often very distinct.

Intertidal zonation is governed in part by the tides: the higher on the shore a plant or animal lives, the more time it spends out of the water. During the summer, longer exposure to air can result in higher body temperatures and increased water loss. The upper distributional limits of many intertidal creatures are set by how well they can withstand heat and desiccation. The lower limits of organisms are often determined by biological factors—other animals or plants that either eat or displace them. At any given site, it takes both clever experimentation and long-term observation to discover the causes of zonation. Nevertheless, the ubiquity of such strong patterns has made the study of this phenomenon a unifying theme in marine ecology.

Plate 6 shows the striking zonation at Tatoosh Island, Washington, in 1982. A 1998 photograph of the same site is nearly identical (and thus not included here), even down to the gulls perching on some favored rocks. This remarkable similarity implies a measure of constancy and local predictability. Plate 104 also illustrates these conspicuous patterns.

Although we use the term *intertidal zone* as an address for these organisms, this designation is often not accurate on wave-swept shores where many species flourish well above the maximum tidal height predicted from tide tables, their vertical distribution extended by wave splash. For instance, tide tables predict a maximum water height of about +3 meters (approximately 10 feet) for the outer coast of Washington. In Plate 6, the white band of the barnacle *Balanus glandula* is at about +4.6 meters, or 15 feet, and in nearby but more exposed sites, at +6.7 meters (22 feet).

Plate 6

P l a t e 7   High intertidal seascape

Biodiversity is reduced on high intertidal platforms like this one. Barnacles (*Balanus glandula*) and especially the golden-brown red alga *Mazzaella cornu-copiae* occupy much of the space.

P l a t e 8   Physiologically stressed algae

Plate 8 depicts middle to high intertidal algae, including *Analipus japonicus* and *Corallina vancouveriensis,* both of which show signs of parching (with *Analipus* turning russet and the *Corallina* white) due to long periods of exposure to sun and lack of immersion by waves.

12

Plate 7

Plate 8

Plate 9   The middle intertidal zone

Plants and animals coexist despite a paucity of available space. Here, a central
group of anemones is surrounded by a variety of algae: the greens are represented by *Ulva* sp.; the browns by the bulbous *Leathesia difformis;* and the reds
by *Microcladia* sp., *Corallina vancouveriensis,* and the fingerlike *Halosaccion
glandiforme.* Some intertidal animal species that have been marked and followed through time attain considerable age: barnacles 1 centimeter (.4 inch)
across may be twelve to thirteen years old; and one giant green sea anemone
was kept in captivity for seventy years. In their natural habitat many sea
anemones are calculated to be at least five hundred years old. Species that
attain great ages and that may take more than a year to mature sexually
have lost the ecological capacity to respond rapidly to changes in their
environment—you might think of them as marine equivalents to giant
sequoia trees. Special care must be taken for their preservation.

Plate 10   Low intertidal diversity

Many plant and animal phyla are represented in Plate 10. Most prominent
are pink coralline algae; with them are sponges, tunicates, starfish, and hydroids. Judged by our terrestrial standards, such evolutionarily based variation
is astonishing.

Plate 9

Plate 10

Plate 11   The lower intertidal

The intertidal brown alga *Laminaria setchellii* belongs to a group commonly referred to as kelps. Also shown in Plate 11 is the green sea grass *Phyllospadix scouleri,* which often forms intertidal meadows.

Low intertidal rocky shores, especially when the shore's slope is gentle, are often characterized by dense stands of plants. Sometimes these are kelps (brown algae), at others true flowering plants (sea grasses). One measure of the extreme significance of nearshore habitats is their contribution to the production of plant matter. Although algal beds, reefs, and estuaries occupy only one-half of 1 percent of the total world ocean area, they contribute a disproportionately high 7 percent of the net primary production (new organic matter produced by photosynthesis), thus serving as the truck farms of the sea. Kelps also get dislodged by storms or have their stipes weakened by grazers; in either instance, they float away from their original attachment site. When shredded into smaller pieces by wave action or cast ashore, they become detritus—an important energy source for other organisms.

Plate 12   *Laminaria setchellii*

Laminaria setchellii produces annual growth rings, which are easily counted when the alga is cross-sectioned: plants examined as beach-cast wrack may be just starting to grow or as old as fifteen years.

ECOLOGICAL INTERACTIONS

An *interaction* occurs when two organisms act on each other in some way. Ecologists interpret such interactions by studying evidence gathered by three different methods: sampling, observing, and experimenting. To understand intertidal zonation, one must find out how many individuals of each different kind

16

Plate 11

Plate 12

of organism live in what kind of places; this can be accomplished by sampling. Then one must look at the animals and plants more closely, to see what the animals eat, how their prey respond, when the organisms reproduce, and when the young appear. But observation alone has proven inadequate to detect the causes of intertidal zonation or to evaluate the ecological roles of individual species in natural assemblages.

Ecologists have begun to understand these natural processes by tampering on a very small scale with the order of nature through experimentation. When such manipulations are scientifically planned, they are based on a comparison between a site left in its natural state (this is called a control) and a site that has been manipulated in some specific fashion. For instance, such experiments may involve the exclusion or addition of a particular predator or competitor, the addition or deletion of refuges, minor modifications of anatomical structures, and even changes in the substratum's color or texture. When properly executed and repeated, such experiments generate precise knowledge of the interactive nature of communities or of how the population of one kind of species is affected by the presence or absence of another. This information is also critically important in managing seashore communities, in predicting the possible effects of human intervention, and in accelerating a community's recovery. Many of the references in the "Further Reading" section refer to such experiments and illustrate how ecologists have reached some of their conclusions about natural patterns and processes.

Plate 13   Interspecific competition

Once a resource becomes limited, organisms will begin to compete for it. In the intertidal zone this resource is usually space. Plate 13 illustrates the sponge *Haliclona* sp. overgrowing barnacles. Clearly, the smaller barnacles will be suffocated and killed; others may avoid this fate by becoming too large to be overgrown, or by having a means of keeping their opercular opening clear.

Plate 14   Predation

Plate 14 depicts an interaction between two species: the starfish *Pisaster ochraceus* is attacking a gooseneck barnacle, *Pollicipes polymerus*. By eating goose barnacles, starfish can keep the lower intertidal free of them, thus helping to maintain zonation patterns.

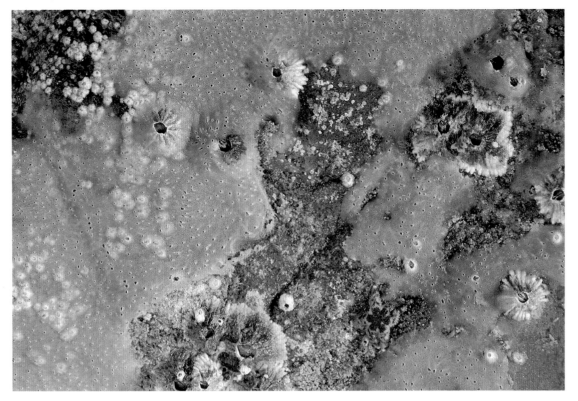

Plate 13

Plate 14

Plate 15   Natural surge channel transformed into a waste-cluttered
junkyard

Plate 16   A normal intertidal channel with sea urchins, anemones,
starfish, and hydrocorals, under a canopy of the kelp *Laminaria setchellii*

The choice of seascapes is ours; humanity does have options. Pristine shores of
all kinds offer an esthetic and biological delight. But they are readily altered when
we dump waste and despoil the seascape or when we change the natural biological composition by introducing unwanted species or deleting others (see
Chapter 6).

The importance of maintaining the integrity and grandeur of the shore cannot be overemphasized, for its intrinsic qualities continue to nurture and sus-
tain our lives. Besides conveying some of the fragility, complexity, and interde-
pendence of the plants and animals that live between the tides along one of the
world's most spectacular coastlines, with this book we hope to portray a place
with its own special beauty, where the subtleties are infinite and kaleidoscopic
and where gazing into a tidepool brings magic. This planet we inhabit is a watery one; only in the intertidal can we be in the worlds of both land and sea at
once. An ethereal and powerful meld of primal elements—solid rock, moving
water, and life itself, sometimes enveloped in fog and other times brilliantly
alight—the intertidal wilderness will always find a way to stir our senses.
Whether or not you have direct access to the shore and its unique beauty, we
hope you will see it through this book as a place to find new meaning.

The following chapters illustrate some of the myriad patterns characteristic
of exposed shorelines and provide clues to interpreting the underlying causal
processes. When you visit the shore, keep in mind that no two areas are identical in topography or inhabitants. Each intertidal site has a flavor and texture of
its own. And just as the composition of species varies from place to place and
time to time, so does the relative intensity of and balance between the many interactions that affect adjacent and associated organisms. Remember, too, that
you will not see all the intertidal treasures in any one excursion. Some of these
organisms are elusive, the patterns subtle. A great part of the allure in any wilderness, however, is the prospect of exploration. Most important, don't let patterns
and scenarios described in these pages stop you from making your own observations on the shore and your own discoveries of its powerful abstract beauty.

Plate 15

Plate 16

2

Competition:

The Struggle for Limited Resources

Organisms have similar and overlapping needs for the basic requisites of life: a place to live, secure refuges, adequate food, and in the case of plants, light. If demand for a particular resource exceeds supply, the resource becomes a limiting factor that induces competition. Since this interaction is of basic importance to understanding the subtle dynamics of any rocky shore, it is necessary to make some fundamental distinctions. When members of a single species are vying—for instance, when hermit crabs of the same species compete for shells in which to live—the quarrel is called *intraspecific*. If two or more species are involved, the competition is *interspecific*.

Competition itself falls into two major categories, though the distinctions between them are sometimes blurred. When the limiting resource is defended by one of the participants or when any direct contact is made, we are witnessing *interference competition*, the most common mode of intertidal competition. Living space is a resource that can be defended, particularly by sessile, permanently attached, organisms, and most of the competitive interactions described below fall into this category. Moreover, because on rocky shores the limiting resource (space) is easily identified and the organisms are often large and observable, many classic ecological studies on competition have been performed in this habitat.

The other kind of competitive interaction is called *exploitation competition*, which involves a mutual striving for a resource that is not defensible. This type occurs, for instance, when one species in the course of depleting its food supply reduces the probability of another species obtaining it. No direct contact between the participants is necessary, and the more efficient species should win eventually. Competition for food by mobile species provides examples of this interaction, the clearest of which involve small organisms inhabiting the open sea, where resource defense is difficult if not impossible.

These definitions refer to ideal conditions and are often applied only with real difficulty to the natural world. For example, on rocky shores, mussels and barnacles live attached to the rock surface and feed on suspended particles brought to them by the water. In this example both food and space are potentially limiting, although marine ecologists generally judge space to be of greater immediate importance, because the organisms can influence its overall availability. In these open communities where large volumes of flowing water continually bring food items to sessile, filter-feeding animals, probably enough for all of them to meet their needs, it is unlikely that competition for food among them is either commonplace or generally important.

Competition has a potent effect on evolution, influencing organisms' distribution, behavior, morphologies, and reproductive strategies. One way for an animal to avoid competitive destruction is to live somewhere in the intertidal zone where its competitors cannot survive. This explanation is often invoked where similar species using resources in a comparable fashion do not overlap spatially. Thus, some barnacles live high in the intertidal zone and others low down. Two or more similar, mobile species that overlap in distribution may eat different prey, as can be observed in nudibranchs. Does this explain their coexistence? Some species are "weedy": they are adept at invading space but, once there, do not persist. Many examples of this phenomenon can be found in seasonally abundant algae. Are they avoiding competition by being biologically active when a dominant species is inactive?

The evidence of competition for space is easily identified on rocky shores. You might find sharp intraspecific or interspecific boundaries; injured tissue along contact lines between species; or even interspecific crushing, crowding, undercutting, or overgrowth, as with barnacles. You might also see regular spacing, as though some constant interaction determined the distance between individuals— as with limpets or some large algal species. One has only to examine the underside of an algal holdfast to find a miniature graveyard of other species that have been overgrown. The ability to acquire, usurp, or guard the spatial resource is often easy to recognize in sessile species, since brute force seems to be their primary tactic. It is possible to see clashes between motile species, such as fish or limpets, as well, though these are difficult to interpret and can express other types of interaction, such as predation.

Ecological wisdom suggests that space is the principal limiting resource for many intertidal species. The availability of refuges from predation can also be important, and the influences of varying amounts and kinds of food have barely been examined. Hence there is still room for alternative explanations of the ways numerous species coexist or why some shores are richer in species than others. The following pages show that mutual striving for common resources is observable in rocky intertidal habitats where interference competition is often graphic.

Plate 17   Space utilization on exposed rock wall

Most or all of the space depicted in Plate 17 is occupied by a wide variety of plant and animal species with different morphologies, life histories, and strategies for competition. This is why real-estate hassles are such a fundamental consideration in understanding rocky shores. On this rock wall, toward the top, a dense aggregation of the acorn barnacle, *Balanus glandula,* lives attached directly to the rock surface. The band's continuity is broken only occasionally by clusters of goose barnacles, *Pollicipes polymerus.* At the midtide level, *Balanus* inhabit a different surface: the shells of the California mussel, *Mytilus californianus.* Still lower, where the sea star *Pisaster ochraceus* consumes mussels, other species, including the alga *Laminaria setchellii,* flourish.

24

Plate 17

Plate 18   Interspecific competition for space between sea anemones, *Anthopleura xanthogrammica,* and a sponge, *Haliclona permollis*

Although little free space remains, the interactions shown here may be benign, allowing the status quo to persist for decades. That is, the sponges cannot overgrow the fleshy, flexible anemones, and the anemones may lack a mechanism to effectively destroy sponges.

Plate 19   Spatial saturation and interspecific competition

Conspicuous in this view are a chiton, sea anemone, barnacles, tunicates, and algae. The photograph shows near-total utilization of space in the lower intertidal zone of coastal Alaska, conditions under which competition among species is bound to occur.

26

Plate 18

Plate 19

Plate 20   Anemone's aggressive response

In an act of reciprocal aggressions, these anemones, *Anthopleura elegantis-sima,* are in the process of stinging their neighbor. The white-tipped tentacles, called acrorhagi, are loaded with stinging cells (nematocysts) and are these animals' weapons of intraspecific competition.

Plate 21   Clonal boundary

Anthopleura elegantissima usually exist as contiguous aggregations of geneti-cally identical individuals, or clones. When alarmed, they will either totally contract or, to defend themselves against intruders, inflate their acrorhagi. Clone mates aren't aggressive to each other but will use their acrorhagi to injure genetically different individuals. One can often see this response exhibited in aggregations, as in Plate 21. A subtle feature of intertidal zones where this species abounds is well-demarcated borders between adjacent clones. These anemone-free strips, once thought to be limpet highways, are now known to be the product of intraspecific competition for space.

28

Plate 20

Plate 21

Plate 22   Hydrocoral territorial stalemate

When two sessile organisms come into contact with each other, at least three outcomes are possible. If the individuals are members of the same species, they may fuse, as do some sponges; in other circumstances the boundary may remain stable, in a sort of stalemate; or the boundary between two organisms may shift in favor of one or the other, depending on which is the superior competitor. Plate 22 shows a discrete boundary between two colonies of the hydrocoral *Allopora californica,* each a clone of genetically identical individuals. Such boundaries are commonplace in this species and are thought to be maintained by interclonal aggression. They usually appear to represent a stalemate, with continuity between the clones maintained but neither one successfully displacing the other. In general, such boundaries indicate that the resource is being divided, but unless one follows them through time, one can't know what the future holds for either participant.

Plate 23   An interpretational dilemma

Plate 23 represents a typical midshore assemblage in coastal Alaska, including the chiton *Katharina tunicata;* a barnacle, *Semibalanus cariosus;* and the sponge *Halichondria panicea.* All the space is occupied. So, is interspecific competition occurring between the mobile chitons and the sessile barnacles, or only between the chitons and the limpets—or, more conspicuously, between the entirely sessile barnacles and the sponges?

Plate 22

Plate 23

Plate 24   Hermit crabs

As part of their life style, hermit crabs require shells. Aggression and ritualized signaling often occur when hermit crabs of the same or different species compete for this limiting resource. The shells they carry serve several essential functions, including protection, for unlike other crabs, these animals have soft abdomens. Their need for bigger homes as they grow continually promotes competitive interactions. In shell contests, the smaller of two hermit crabs is made to abandon its shell, allowing the bigger crab to examine its adequacy. Often this is achieved by behavioral signaling, which attains the same end result, but without brute force, and minimizes the danger of physical damage to the participants. Thus, if the bigger crab wants a new home, a shell exchange will take place. If not, the owners each reclaim their original shells. In Plate 24, a *Pagurus samuelis* occupying a *Tegula* shell is initiating an examination of a *Calliostoma* shell inhabited by a smaller member of the same species.

32

Plate 25   Mobile consumers (an urchin, limpet, hermit crabs, and brittle stars) in a mussel bed

Interspecific competition for space is readily observed in both Plates 24 and 25. Determining even the presence of resource competition, let alone its outcome, among these mobile consumers is an ecological challenge. Direct observation may reveal few clues, and mobility makes the participants difficult study subjects. Such restrictions do not apply to sessile species, as the following photographs illustrate.

Plate 24

Plate 25

Plate 26   Hydrocoral and coralline algae

In the intertidal zone, one finds animals in vigorous competition for space with plants. Plate 26 shows *Pseudolithophyllum muricatum,* a dynamic competitor among the coralline algae, overgrowing the bright pink, pitted skeletons of the colonial animal *Allopora californica.* The relationships between *Allopora* and other species of coralline algae, however, are less clear.

Plate 27   Barnacles

Barnacles in general show a well-defined hierarchy of competitive abilities, with the larger species in a confrontation crushing, overgrowing, or undercutting the smaller. Don't be surprised, however, if you find reversals. Smaller species will occasionally outcompete a larger one, although these incidents are rare. Plate 27 illustrates some *Balanus glandula* overgrowing individuals of the smaller, browner barnacle *Chthamalus dalli.* In other encounters, *B. glandula* appears to have modified its usually circular outline and grown around the *Chthamalus.* Perhaps the differences result from variations in individual size at the time of initial contact.

At other places along the shore, one can find barnacle hummocks. When these animals are numerous and space is at a premium, the crowding individuals inadvertently squeeze one another, becoming more columnar in shape as they grow. Individual barnacles characterized by this unstable growth form are more susceptible to being swept off the rocks.

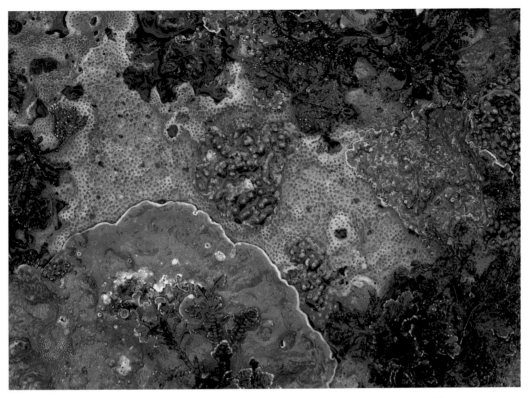

Plate 26

Plate 27

Plates 28 and 29   Beds of the mussel *Mytilus californianus*

On the exposed rocky shores from San Francisco to British Columbia, the dominant intertidal competitor is the mussel *Mytilus californianus.* Left to their own devices, without interruption or interference from physical disturbance or predation, mussels are capable of monopolizing the substratum by smothering other primary-space occupiers, rendering the space uninhabitable to more mobile species, or presenting a phalanx of sharp edges against which waves shred competing kelps.

Mussels attach by byssal fibers secreted by a gland at the base of the foot. These slender, flexible threads can be voluntarily dissolved by the mussel and new fiber produced, giving mussels the mobility necessary both to move onto new space and to reclaim terrain lost to the ravages of physical disturbance. This ability might explain the competitive dominance of mussels in many rocky intertidal communities worldwide.

Mussel beds, which can grow up to 40 centimeters (15 inches) thick, are composed of many strata, making the habitat an enormously variegated and reticulated world of sheltered openings. This specialized habitat supplies space to a seemingly endless number of hangers-on, many of which are too small to be easily seen (see Plate 25). Organic debris and fecal matter accumulate here as well, providing a rich soup for deposit and suspension feeders. Such unbroken stands may look like a monoculture, since this life form would appear to be excluding others. On the other hand, if one's frame of reference were the mussel bed itself, the bed and its associated community would be described biologically as an extremely rich assemblage.

No organism in any natural community can survive as a jack of all trades, master of none; if a species excels in one vital ecological function, a vulnerability elsewhere can be assumed. Mussels eventually pay a price for their competitive superiority; as they become larger, they also become more vulnerable to the shearing forces of wave action.

Plate 30   Goose barnacles in outwash

Although goose barnacles (*Pollicipes polymerus*) lose in competition with mussels on horizontal surfaces, they apparently thrive on vertical walls. This position helps them to filter prey from wave runoff, which they are doing here. Severe wave action and high water velocity bring food to goose barnacles, at the same time protecting them from mussels, whose byssal fibers function less efficiently on walls.

Plate 28

Plate 29

Plate 30

Plates 31 and 32   The varied faces of competition

Plate 31 illustrates a hierarchical arrangement of species, with the sponge *Halichondria* sp. overgrowing the barnacle *Semibalanus cariosus*, and both of these overgrowing two kinds of crustose coralline algae. Within the latter, the darker purple crust, *Pseudolithophyllum muricatum*, is overgrowing the very thin species *P. whidbeyense*. Such hierarchical competitive arrangements seem certain to lead to spatial monopolies.

However, straightforward interpretation is often clouded by competitive reversals, as Plate 32 illustrates. In this situation, most of the space is occupied by the bryozoan *Cryptosula* sp. and the sponge *Haliclona permollis*, each of which can be seen overgrowing the other. One of the issues of interest to marine biologists today is whether competitive interactions are linear and their outcomes predictable, as in the hierarchy in Plate 31, or whether they are arranged in complex networks or loops, with no single species being the winner for more than a relatively brief instant because the relationships are constantly in flux. In networks of competition, all the involved species persist because no one species is capable of dominating all the others.

Plate 33   Sea palms (*Postelsia palmaeformis*) overgrowing mussels, barnacles, and smaller algae

Plate 34   A tube worm and coralline algae

Not only is the rock substrate thick with life, but often the organisms themselves are festooned with other plants and animals. Many species are what we call secondary-space occupiers, either by close association or because of lack of other or better choices. Plants and animals growing attached to other plants are called *epiphytic;* on animals they are *epizoic;* and a more general term including both is *epibiont.* The well-being of their hosts directly influences their own. Thus, environmental stresses on the host inevitably affect the guest. In Plate 34, a calcareous tube worm, *Serpula vermicularis,* is both growing on coralline algal crusts and serving as surface for them. Epibiont seems the simplest term to apply to such complex relationships.

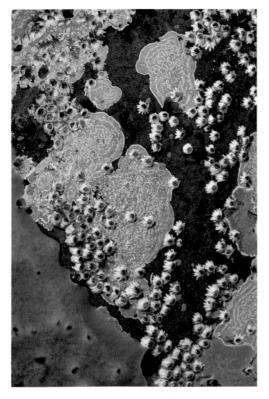

Plate 31

Plate 32

Plate 33

Plate 34

Plate 35   Epiphytic coralline algae

Plate 36   Sponge and barnacles

Overgrowth relationships are not always antagonistic. Some interactions between two or more species living together in close physical proximity benefit all parties. Or, if only one gains, it will be at no cost to the others. Such relationships have traditionally been termed mutualisms or symbioses. They have always caught the eye of both naturalists and ecologists, whom they continue to vex.

A fine example is provided by the giant barnacle *Balanus nubilus* and the sponge *Halichondria panicea,* which are often associated, as in Plate 36. *B. nubilus* is one of the largest acorn barnacles on the west coast of North America and normally is subtidal, but it may grow intertidally on wave-exposed points. *H. panicea,* distinguished by both its odor and texture, has a cosmopolitan distribution and varies in shape and color. Each can exist without the other.

Substantial experimental evidence indicates that sponges benefit their hosts. We know that sponge cover markedly reduces the ability of tube feet to adhere and thus can reduce predation by starfish. But does the barnacle do anything to attract the sponge? For the sponge, what advantages are conferred other than a suitable settlement site? Does it share the feeding current of the host, thereby gaining an additional supply of nutrients? Are *B. nubilus*'s extremely hooked beaks a morphological adaptation for pruning back and preventing complete overgrowth by encrusting species such as *Halichondria*?

One species garners protection by being associated with the second. The second gains more space on which to live. Is this accidental, or has each made reciprocal modifications and sacrifices to further and maintain the partnership?

Plate 37   Green algae atop a limpet

The shell of the limpet *Notoacmaea scutum* bears tufts of a filamentous green alga, *Cladophora* sp., which can also be found growing on the rock substratum. It is not known whether the alga occupies this mobile surface as a refuge, as a preferred habitat, or by necessity as a suboptimal site.

40

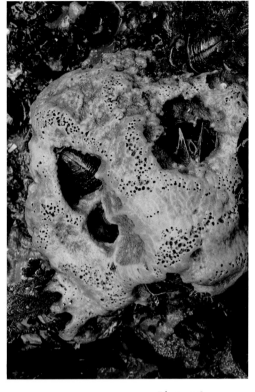

Plate 35

Plate 36

Plate 37

Plate 38   Wind-blown waves

Conditions like these, in which salt water is blown well above the tide's technical upper limit, help nurture dense populations of algae and barnacles and thereby ensure a rich mix of ecological processes even at supra-tidal levels.

42

Plate 38

3

Predation

Along the Pacific coast of North America, predator-prey interactions appear to be of particular consequence to the structure of intertidal communities. Predation governs the distribution of many intertidal organisms and suggests that their colors, shapes, and behaviors reflect the urgent need to avoid being attacked or consumed.

Predation is the act of eating or preying upon plants or animals by other animals. This process commonly and effectively removes individuals from the substratum, thereby creating space or other resources for different species. Sometimes, though, the prey is only nibbled or partially consumed, and many marine organisms survive these encounters, eventually regenerating lost parts. In the intertidal zone one can see some predators seeking or eating their prey, but the activities of others are usually revealed only by such circumstantial evidence as bite marks, grazing trails, or the virtual absence of prey species from areas where their predators normally roam.

Consumers are grouped by their characteristic food choices into generalized categories called trophic levels: herbivore and carnivore are two common ones, depending on whether the food is plant or animal. Other species, called omnivores, aren't as easily categorized and may consume a wider range of "prey," including carrion and detritus. All three groups ultimately depend on the food energy fixed during photosynthesis by plants, or producers.

When we examine the feeding relationships within a whole community, we find a natural hierarchical order in the predation process. To describe this, ecologists have developed the concept of food webs, in which plants are consumed by herbivores, which in turn are consumed by carnivores. This more abstract, less observable ecological framework is necessary to describe the resulting flow of energy through a community, but it does not explain the ecological influences of a particular species. Further, predator-prey relationships are thought to be fundamental to understanding the stability or persistence of natural communities, an aspect of major significance as human beings gradually alter most biological communities, including those on the shore.

Predators often play dramatic and important roles, although the visual evidence of their effects occurs on a less grand scale than some forms of disturbance. For instance, a predator might reduce the numbers of an effective competitor, such as mussels that are capable of dominating an area. The liberated space can then be invaded by the marine equivalent of weeds: animal and plant species that require disruption of the status quo and occupy the space only temporarily. This dynamic suggests the counterintuitive conclusion that modest predation may lead to more diverse assemblages, since freedom from biological disruption yields ecological monotony. For this reason, perhaps, intertidal communities along exposed shorelines are among the more diverse known.

Predation is fundamentally involved in explanations of the fabric of nature. Of the three methods of scientific inquiry discussed in the introduction, observation and experimentation have yielded rich data on predation. Some species are absent or rare in what seems to be acceptable habitat. The observed presence of a highly effective predator may explain why. Experiments have demonstrated that local community appearance can change rapidly following quite subtle shifts in the consumer population. Such demonstrations have enormous implications for applied ecology and the management of our seashore resources, since they show that certain species have an importance out of proportion to their local abundance.

Predation is a conspicuous event and often leaves striking evidence of its occurrence. Many animals are active feeders only during high tide, at other times retreating under rocks, into crevices, or among dense algae, where they remain inactive. However, receding tides often reveal natural acts of predation in progress, especially when it takes the predator more than one tidal cycle to consume the prey. Subtler forms of ecological evidence may also be present: grazed trails, drilled holes, or chipped shells, to name a few. Their presence provides irrefutable evidence that some consumer passed that way, nibbling, browsing, destroying. Finally, the design features of intertidal organisms become especially noteworthy in the context of predation. Morphological traits such as shell thickness in mussels, the structure of barnacle plates, or even the shape of limpets all suggest adaptations to minimize the chance that they will be eaten. They reflect the continuing contest between predator and prey, with the goal being the avoidance of becoming "lunch" for some successful consumer.

It is possible to interpret behavioral and chemical prey defenses, which include poisonous secretions, noxious taste, pinching, biting, and color, as means evolved to frustrate the efforts of predators. In addition, ecologists think that vulnerable species, or species susceptible to being consumed, increase their survival chances by being highly seasonal or by showing up in unpredictable places, thus escaping in time or space. Conversely, less tangible predator attributes such as long-range chemosensory abilities, acute eyesight, and swiftness have all evolved to enhance an organism's ability to exploit some resource. Although this evolutionary game of hide and seek, often likened to an "arms race," is ubiquitous, there are excellent reasons for believing that such features serve a variety of purposes. The ribbing on a massive shell, for example, could make the animal more immune to drilling, or could prevent it from being dislodged by wave action. The following pages illustrate many such observable aspects of the predation process, a process that is a vital part of the cycling and turnover of resources within the intertidal zone and that generates fascinating ecological complexities.

Plate 39 Wave-carved seascape

Tatoosh Island, Washington, is the nesting site of many birds. Gulls are probably the most important predator of the goose barnacles *Pollicipes polymerus*. Another species characteristic of and unique to our rocky shores, the black oystercatcher, consumes large numbers of limpets, mussels, littorines, and sea urchins. Look for the hallmarks of their predation: limpet shells with broken edges or sea urchins with their spines neatly removed from around the Aristotle's lantern area.

46

Plate 39

Plate 40   Periwinkles and their algal prey

The small herbivorous snail *Littorina sitkana* grazes on the alga *Enteromorpha* sp. Many species, including these, are called generalists: they have broad feeding habits and eat a variety of prey without showing marked preferences. Others are specialists: they feed on a single or few prey.

Plate 41   A grazing trail

In Plate 41, a telltale trail has been produced in a diatomaceous mat as a grazing limpet rasped its way back and forth. Limpets, littorines, and chitons all influence the microflora, and with practice it is possible to distinguish the feeding marks of these major groups. Although it may appear detrimental, the grazing of certain species is important, because diatoms or other small algae in abundance can smother the surface. Also, if sporelings survive and grow to become larger algae, they can outcompete the species on which they initially settled. An interesting byproduct of these feeding activities is that they remove particles of rock as well; grain by grain, grazers are capable of deepening tidepools by 1 centimeter (.2 inch) every sixteen years. In general, animals that feed by rasping and scraping can wear away rock at a rate equal to that of other erosive processes such as exfoliation, chemical solution, or physical abrasion. Thus, when a population is abundant, the erosion resulting from its feeding activities is appreciable.

Plate 42   Communal feeding on drift kelp

An aggregation of *Littorina sitkana* is feeding on a detached frond of *Nereocystis* brought within their reach by waves. A single snail probably couldn't anchor the drifting mass, but groups can. This leads one to consider the many possible functions of a snail's shell: to protect the animal from predators, rolling rocks, and desiccation, and to aid in anchoring drifting kelp.

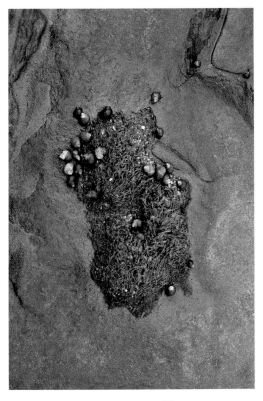

Plate 40

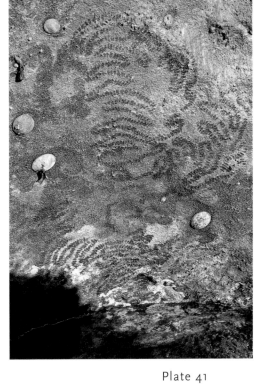

Plate 41

Plate 42

Plate 43   Sea urchin–dominated seascape

Purple sea urchins, *Strongylocentrotus purpuratus,* exert a tremendous influence on the diversity and abundance of intertidal flora: they can graze a garden of kelp down to a pavement of pink crustose coralline algae. The aggregation of sea urchins in Plate 43 almost totally controls the character of the plant community. The herd pictured is in a traditional spot for sea urchins and was there for at least fifteen years until eliminated by sea otters in about 1990 (see Chapter 6).

Sea urchins feed while immersed, using an apparatus known as an Aristotle's lantern, which is equipped with intricate and efficient jaws for nibbling and scraping food, and perhaps for excavating burrows. Plate 44 shows the star-spangled bite marks of a sea urchin on a piece of kelp. One can argue that sea urchin grazing activities are advantageous to the understory coralline algae, for the urchins protect these algae from being overgrown by diatoms or fleshy plants. Crustose algae are usually colorful and serve as an excellent indicator of intense grazing pressure at all latitudes. In fact, the predominance of coralline algae in many tropical communities is an accepted hallmark of herbivorous fish activity.

Sea urchins play a major role in the organization of subtidal as well as intertidal communities. Factors influencing their activities vitally affect the benthic algal community. Thus, the presence of sea otters, which eat sea urchins, can make possible lush forests of kelp that urchins would otherwise decimate. The removal of sea urchins, whether by otters in California and the Aleutians or by people and the sunflower starfish, *Pycnopodia helianthoides,* in Washington and Alaska, always produces dramatic changes.

50

Plate 43

Plate 44   Sea urchin grazing marks

Plate 45   Limpet and coralline algae

Plate 45 illustrates evidence of grazing on a pink coralline crust, where a species that tends to feed selectively on this resource, the limpet *Acmaea mitra,* has browsed it practically down to bedrock. The lined chiton, *Tonicella lineata* (see Plate 96), also feeds on coralline algae; however, very few other animals graze on these rocklike red algae, whose tissues are enmeshed in a matrix of calcium carbonate. The scraping organ, or radula, of these two grazing species is considerably harder than that of many other grazers and functions as a combination rasp and conveyor belt. Ecologically, the radula may be suited to a very specific kind of food, thus restricting what the grazer can eat.

Many *Acmaea mitra,* unlike other limpets, are encrusted with coralline algae. In Plate 45 the encrusting alga, *Pseudolithophyllum whidbeyense,* is reproductive: the small white dots on the limpet's back are the alga's reproductive structures. Intertidal ecologists have found that a higher proportion of reproductive crusts are found on the backs of limpets than on the rock substratum. Although the encrustation may serve to camouflage the limpet, it is also possible that the safest place for the alga to be is riding piggyback on one of its major consumers.

Plate 46   The bat star, *Asterina miniata*

These starfish feed on a wide range of items in a remarkable variety of ways. When their stomachs are extended, they could be scavenging, digesting detrital materials, consuming recently settled larvae, or even suspension feeding.

52

Plate 44

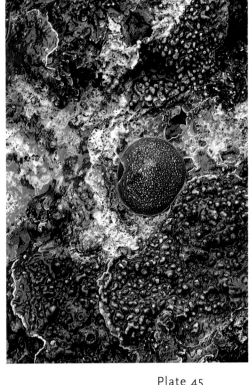

Plate 45

Plate 46

Plates 47 and 48   Whelks and their prey, mussels and barnacles

Small round holes in the shells of the mussel *Mytilus trossulus* (formerly
M. edulis) are a sure sign that the animals were eaten by a shell-boring snail,
such as *Nucella canaliculata* (Plate 47). Irregular holes could be drilled by
octopus. *Nucella* spends one to two days drilling and consuming this prey.
It makes a small, circular hole with its filelike radula and a shell-dissolving
enzymatic acidic secretion, and then inserts its proboscis and rasps out the
prey's soft tissues. Predation of this sort seems to be limited to thinner-
shelled organisms; larger barnacles and mussels appear to be immune
by virtue of their body size. *Nucella* also eats small barnacles, *Semibalanus
cariosus* (Plate 48), although these are not usually drilled.

54

Plate 47

Plate 48

Plate 49   Starfish predation

The ochre starfish, *Pisaster ochraceus,* sits characteristically humped up over its favorite prey, the mussel *Mytilus californianus.* This starfish is a generalist carnivore, feeding on barnacles, chitons, goose barnacles, and limpets as well as mussels by inserting a part of its stomach into the prey. Once the prey is subdued, it is lifted or yanked from the substratum and tightly applied against the starfish's oral surface, where it may be almost totally enveloped in the stomach's folds.

The foraging behavior of *Pisaster* involves a vertical movement: the animals move upward during high tide to capture prey, and often return to a lower tidepool or surge-channel refuge to digest it. The upper limit of their effective foraging is conspicuously marked by a browse line, which likewise identifies the lower limit of mussel and barnacle populations.

Sea anemones, *Anthopleura xanthogrammica,* are often found near mussel beds, in effect waiting in the wings for a meal generated in part by *Pisaster*'s feeding activities. The anemones, in fact, settled in the mussel bed as larvae and later worked their way downward, flourishing from proximity and association with the starfish.

This starfish has been referred to as a *keystone species* because it exerts a strong and disproportionate influence on the community's structure through its feeding activities, preferentially consuming a prey that could otherwise dominate the space. Like wave-generated physical disturbance, predation restrains or removes one species, making possible an increase in others that require surfaces for attachment.

Plate 49

Plate 50   Fish ambush

Predators have different tactics for obtaining prey. Some are slow and creeping in their attack, others chase. Some sit and wait but have to conceal themselves while they lie in ambush, since their prey would recognize and avoid them if possible. In Plate 50 the smooth-head sculpin, *Artedius lateralis*, common in tidepools and shallow waters, has ambushed a prey item, *Jordania zanope*, a juvenile long-fin sculpin.

Plate 51   Sea anemone predation

The sea anemone *Anthopleura xanthogrammica* waits for the waves to bring it food or for prey to wander fortuitously within reach, as was probably the case with the crab, *Oedignathus* sp., in Plate 51. Many crabs disappear down anemone gullets and are later strewn out as bits of shell after strong enzymes have digested the body parts. These anemones derive the majority of their diet from food swept to them by the waves, particularly uprooted mussels that may have been loosened by foraging gulls or starfish before the waves knocked them free. Thus, anemones are among the major beneficiaries of disruptive wave action, catching these morsels as they fall out of eddying water and moving them to their mouths with tentacles. The ring of tentacles surrounding the mouth is packed with nematocysts, minute stinging structures with microscopic barbs, which are used for defense and food capture. As wave action diminishes, so does the average body size and abundance of *A. xanthogrammica*. This is why one finds them living in places of maximum water flow, often carpeting the bottom of surge channels.

Plate 50

Plate 51

Plate 52   Tentaculate consumers

Organisms have evolved numerous techniques for extracting prey from the
marine world. For instance, sponges and mussels pump food-carrying water
across filtering organs. Pictured here are an anemone that actively catches
prey with tentacles, taking detritus, marine larvae, and zooplankton; and a
fan worm that uses cilia and mucus to obtain even smaller particles.

Plate 53   Nudibranch and hydroid

Nudibranchs such as *Coryphella trilineata* usually feed on hydroids, such as
the *Eudendrium* sp. shown in Plate 53. Amphipods sitting on hydroids have
been observed attacking and successfully repelling climbing nudibranchs, in
the process protecting the hydroid from one of its major consumers. Three-
party interactions such as this are challenging to interpret: are they merely a
coincidence or is there substantive biological meaning to them? The amphipod might be protecting its habitat from destruction. If so, it would benefit
hydroids to somehow attract amphipods. In nature's open market, where
protection, housing, and feeding are exchangeable commodities, "barters"
between species are an established practice and can lead to mutual benefit.

Plate 54   A sea spider, *Pycnogonum stearnsi*

Along with starfish, nudibranchs, and a few fish, pycnogonids, or sea spiders,
are one of the few animals to eat sea anemones. Sea spiders are typically found
burrowed into the column of an anemone, where they feed by inserting their
proboscis.

Plate 52

Plate 53

Plate 54

Plates 55 and 56   Plant chemical defense

Antipredator defenses are well documented in terrestrial plants and include tannins in the leaves of oaks, the poison of poison ivy, and digitalis in foxglove. The brown alga *Desmarestia* sp. produces sulphuric acid in small cavities, which leak when the alga is damaged. Plate 55 shows *Desmarestia* lying atop other algae; Plate 56 shows the bleaching effect the sulphuric acid has had on the underlying plants. The living plant is eaten by few invertebrates, but it isn't known whether the sulphuric acid functions in defense against predators or in competition for space with other organisms, particularly plants. It probably serves both ends, deterring grazing and giving the alga a competitive edge.

Plate 57   Keyhole limpet

Rather than running away from starfish as many limpets do, the common keyhole limpet *Diodora aspera* frustrates the efforts of its predators by responding proactively to their proximity or contact. The limpet raises itself off the substrate, extending part of its mantle over its shell and another part downward. This leaves no ready place where the starfish can fasten its tube feet, thus increasing the probability that the limpet will escape.

Plate 55

Plate 56

Plate 57

P l a t e 5 8   By-the-wind sailor, *Velella velella*

These animals, pelagic relatives of hydroids and anemones, are often seen floating at the surface in offshore waters. They are also at the mercy of winds and are often cast ashore in large numbers. As food items, they can be important in the diet of sessile intertidal organisms such as the sea anemone *Anthopleura elegantissima*. A study in Alaska showed that when huge quantities of another kind of gelatinous zooplankton washed ashore, sea urchins shifted their diet to this novel prey, thereby allowing algae to flourish temporarily. Chance events, or unpredictable opportunities, can alter what we observe.

6 4

Plate 58

4

Reproduction and Settlement on the Shore

Reproduction is of obvious importance if species are to replace their dead, increase in numbers, or extend their geographical distribution, and it occurs by a startling variety of methods. Natural selection favors the traits of those organisms whose offspring survive to become reproductive, which explains the interest of ecologists in all phases of reproductive biology. Not surprisingly, it is more than just the number of offspring produced by a female that renders her the fittest. One must consider the health and vigor of the offspring and thus their probability of surviving to reproduce, since they will be the bearers of her genes. With birds, it has been shown that in harsh years individuals producing fewer eggs are favored over those attempting to raise larger families. The moral is that fewer is sometimes better. For marine invertebrates in which the clutch size is naturally limited and/or parental care such as brooding is involved, the same constraints against increasingly large clutch sizes probably apply.

When thousands or even millions of eggs are produced, as in many marine organisms, another type of reasoning is required, since reducing the "clutch" from, for example, one million fifteen to one million is not apt to make much difference. Many species producing large numbers of larvae have great adult longevity but also experience highly variable recruitment success. A long reproductive life ensures that occasionally the repopulation process will be successful: it might be called a boom-or-bust strategy. Another characteristic reproductive pattern involves those species whose individuals reproduce only once and then die. Pacific salmon and octopus are examples. The reasons underlying this reproductive strategy are thought to involve a very reduced probability of an individual surviving to reproduce twice. In all cases, natural selection favors the genetic traits of the individuals producing the most surviving offspring.

Reproduction includes two major modes: *asexual,* as in budding, transverse fission, or fragmentation, in which no recombination of genetic material takes place; and *sexual,* in which gametes from two individuals unite to produce a third. Interestingly, some species combine these possibilities and reap the varying advantages of both modes. For example, the sea anemone *Anthopleura elegantissima* produces large clones of genetically identical individuals by asexual reproduction; however, some also release sperm or eggs that, when fertilized, produce larvae genetically different from both parents and capable of dispersing over a wide distance.

In many marine organisms fertilization is external, with free-living larvae being produced from the vast numbers of sperm and egg that are shed into the water. Many worms and echinoderms, such as our common sea urchins, fall into this category. In others, fertilization occurs internally, with the parent then releasing the larvae into the sea. Barnacles are a familiar example. These life-history patterns are referred to as *indirect development,* since the larvae spend varying intervals of time floating or wandering as plankton in the surface layers of the water before settling to the bottom and adopting adult habits. Other animals lack a free-living larval stage and encapsulate or brood their eggs. A juvenile emerges after metamorphosis and simply crawls away over the rock surface. The snail *Nucella* and the brooding starfish *Leptasterias* reproduce in this fashion. This mode of reproduction, in which a miniature replica of the parent is produced, is known as *direct development.*

For most marine algae and invertebrates, the primary dispersal stage is spores or larvae, morphologically different from their parent and carried unknown distances by water currents. Algal spores probably settle out haphazardly, but the location of newly metamorphosed juvenile invertebrates is often based on decisions made by the larva, so marine ecologists have been interested in a quartet of closely related phenomena: larval development and dispersal, habitat selection, and metamorphosis. The phenomenon of dispersal is universal: it amounts to not putting all one's eggs in a single basket and is therefore a strong hedge against local extinction. A species that spreads itself over a larger landscape not only may encounter suitable, unoccupied habitat but will be much less susceptible to local catastrophes.

The movement of an individual from one location to another, the distance and means of transportation and locomotion, and the life-history stage involved differ markedly among taxonomic groups. There are three benefits to planktonic dispersal: wider genetic exchange, the potential colonization of distant geographic areas, and the ability to take advantage of available habitat. It is very difficult for biologists to trace or identify a particular group of larvae drifting at large in the sea, because plankton are patchy and difficult to mark, making them hard to sample. Consequently, many mysteries remain in this critical process. What is the specific site or population from which particular larvae were derived? How far are they transported by complex coastal currents? How long can they remain in the plankton, delaying metamorphosis if necessary until an appropriate settlement site is found? When development is indirect, the recolonization of intertidal habitats depends on how well the larvae survive the hazards of the planktonic interval. One can't help but marvel that any survive to adulthood, given the many obstacles. One of the challenges of marine biologists' work is to ascertain from the adult distribution whether its positioning was determined by selective settlement, with the larvae exercising a genuine choice, by the chance survival of recruiting larvae, or both.

Larvae have organs for swimming and attachment, and sense organs to prospect for and identify their habitat. Some larvae react to light, gravity, specific chemical substances, or changes in pressure. They swim or drift until sensory cues tell them to settle. When a mobile larva either randomly settles or is enticed to settle on a spot, the process is referred to as *settlement. Metamorphosis,* changes in both morphology and appearance and the habitat in which the individual lives, often occurs during or immediately after settlement. The term *recruitment* is increasingly used to refer to the survival of settled individuals to a size at which they can be accurately identified.

The period spent in landing on a suitable place to live and undergoing metamorphosis preliminary to initiating the postlarval life is critical. Many of the necessary settlement decisions are surprisingly specific. Larvae have some freedom and capacity to recognize and distinguish among different habitats, and therefore they exercise some choice. They may settle in proximity to their own kind, in crevices of a given darkness, in water currents of a given velocity, or with another species with which they have a biotic relationship of some type.

Settling larvae may discriminate between surfaces, preferring, for example, certain kinds of rock over others for reasons that might include the rock's texture, the presence of an appropriate surface film, or conditioning by chemical bleaching. Some living surfaces defend themselves from would-be settlers by mechanical devices or chemical means. For instance, some starfish have pedicellaria—pinching structures useful for protecting their surfaces. Some of the benthic algae may be too smooth to settle on, others may secrete noxious chemicals to in-

68

hibit settlers, and a few shed their surface layers like dandruff, in the process of removing bacteria and spores inhabiting their surfaces.

The precise mechanisms by which larvae test, explore, and crawl about surfaces are not well known, but the fact that some can attach temporarily, or can delay metamorphosis and spend long times in the plankton, suggests that marine animals, unlike dandelion or maple seeds, do not settle at random. Once metamorphosis has been initiated, it is usually completed in a remarkably short time, and immediately afterward the metamorphosed juvenile is faced with a new suite of predators and competitors. The relationship between adults and juveniles can take many forms, with the highly vulnerable juvenile stage being protected in some instances and left to its own devices in others.

Reproduction superbly illustrates many trade-offs and ecological compromises. Small eggs, for example, are metabolically cheaper to manufacture than larger ones, and therefore can be produced in proportionately larger numbers. An egg mass brooded by a parent or laid in a capsule uses more energy, yet is more secure from the vagaries of life than an embryo free-floating in the open sea, though this benefit is bought at the sacrifice of dispersal. Furthermore, the brooding adult may be committed to an interval of voluntary starvation. The timing and place of reproduction can involve similar trade-offs: for instance, an individual that spawns early in the year may increase the probability that its offspring will have first access to optimal settlement sites, but the larvae may encounter unfavorable environmental conditions. Additionally, what may be a secure spawning location for the adults may be a hostile site for the settling larvae.

Considering the enormous variety of reproductive methods, it is impossible not to wonder about the relative advantages of particular strategies. What are the offsetting advantages of sexual versus asexual reproduction, of the sexes being separate or an individual being a true functional hermaphrodite? What is it about the production of egg capsules that might outweigh the advantages of long-distance dispersal? In the case of animals that broadcast gametes, must they be tightly aggregated, and is this an especially important factor for sessile species or those of limited mobility? Observations on adult individuals have provided little help in solving these reproductive quandaries: with some groups, such as limpets and barnacles, one often finds juveniles; in others, such as starfish and sea urchins, the presence of juveniles is much less predictable. These variations and a great many more questions of basic significance continue to intrigue biologists.

69

Plates 59 and 60   Intertidal algae

The life history of benthic marine algae is highly complex, offering to the unsuspecting biologist a maze filled with pitfalls and riddles. Essentially it involves the alternation of a sexual and an asexual generation within any given species (although in some the alternate phase is either unknown or bypassed). These algal generations may be identical morphologically, in which case the species is referred to as *isomorphic*. In other species, one generation may look entirely different from its alternative phase; these algae thus are *heteromorphic*. The latter situation is challenging to phycologists, because if the plant cannot be cultured in the laboratory, there is no guaranteed way to link the two phases. Plates 59 and 60 show, respectively, *Mastocarpus (Gigartina) papillata* and *Petrocelis middendorffii*, the two phases in the life cycle of a single red alga. Morphologically, they are distinctive; they are also very different ecologically. *Petrocelis*, the encrusting asexual form, is perennial and very long lived, apparently attaining ages of over ninety years. *Mastocarpus*, the textured upright blade form, reproduces sexually and is thought to be an annual.

Complexities such as these can have profound economic importance. Many red algae have been traditional food for maritime cultures. Of commercially exploited red algae, *Porphyra*, a food item (*nori*) treasured by the Japanese, is the most familiar. *Porphyra* culture now supports a $2-billion-a-year industry. However, sustained economic yield was not possible until the microscopic alternative phase, *Conchocelis*, was found living subtidally within calcareous rock and clam shells.

70

Plate 59

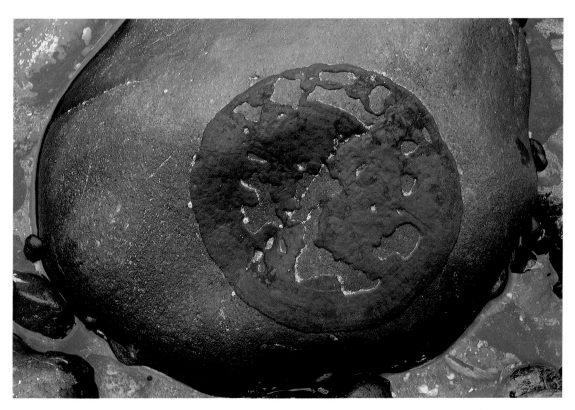

Plate 60

Plate 61   Bull kelp

Plate 62   Beached kelp

Bull kelp, *Nereocystis luetkeana,* is an abundant species of kelp. The conspicuous phase of this annual plant (Plate 61) is one of the largest of brown algae,
attaining lengths in excess of 20 meters (65 feet) in a single season. It is
capable of growing as much as 60 centimeters (23 inches) a day. When the
plant matures, vast numbers of swimming spores are produced and liberated.
These become a cohort of bottom-dwelling microscopic plants, which then
reproduce sexually, yielding in the next generation the massive phase that
forms great forests just offshore. Toward the ends of their lives, the large
plants often become entangled, detaching themselves and each other from
the rock. The holdfast in marine plants only anchors the plant to the bottom;
unlike the roots of most land plants, it does not take up nutrients or water.
Therefore, once torn loose, the plants are still capable of reproduction and
growth, as long as they continue to be exposed to water circulation and light.
As wrack cast up on the shore (Plate 62), they provide food and habitat for
many small organisms. When pulverized into increasingly finer particles,
they may even become food for suspension-feeding barnacles and mussels.

72

Plate 61

Plate 62

Plate 63   Coralline algae and their reproductive structures

In the crustose coralline alga *Pseudolithophyllum muricatum,* the reproductive structures are visible as a field of small white dots. These are called *conceptacles,* fertile cavities opening to the surface of the plant. Coralline algae are isomorphic, meaning that the two alternating generations look alike. The positioning of the conceptacles, whether raised or sunken, is thought to be related to the influence of grazing pressure over evolutionary time. Specific structural variations can discourage herbivores and minimize browsing; the plant may be erect or encrusting and thin or relatively thick, and varying amounts of calcium carbonate may be deposited in its walls. In the tropics, where grazing pressure is even heavier than along the temperate Pacific coast, one can find calcareous brown and green algae as well as red.

Plate 64   Sea grass and seed-bearing shoots

The marine benthic flora is well represented by lower plants: macroscopic algae, benthic diatoms, and blue-green algae (now considered to be bacteria). It also includes fungi, lichens, and the so-called sea grasses, which are most closely allied to the taxonomically more advanced terrestrial plants and actually produce flowers and seeds. *Phyllospadix scouleri* is a perennial sea grass that occurs on wave-swept shores, living attached to rocks or wedged in crevices by means of its creeping rhizomes and roots. This plant has the capacity to swamp out entire tidepools, although, as in mussels, the tendency is thwarted by wave action or other forms of disturbance. *Phyllospadix* produces a shoot bearing seeds, seen in Plate 64; pollination occurs underwater with the help of water currents. *Zostera,* another sea grass, occurs in more protected habitats. Both these plants are important as nursery grounds for economically important fish and crustaceans. When they detach, they are also a major source of organic debris, contributing this material, known as detritus, to distant food webs. *Zostera* rhizomes help stabilize the sediment, and the blades are a vital food source for migrating waterfowl such as brant.

Plate 65   The blood star, *Henricia* sp.

This species of starfish broadcast their gametes; close relatives brood egg masses.

74

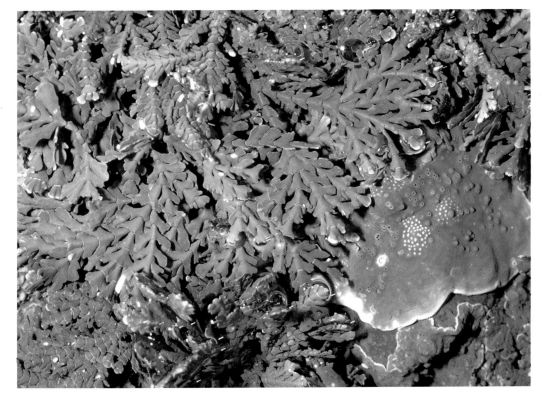

Plate 63

Plate 64

Plate 65

Plate 66   Brooding sea anemone

Epiactis prolifera maintains a sex life unique among animal species. Its young, which are brooded around its base, are not formed by budding but are produced sexually. Eggs of the female parent are fertilized by planktonic sperm in her digestive cavity, where the embryos develop into motile larvae. They then escape through her mouth, glide down, and become embedded in the column, where they remain until the are fully formed and ready to migrate away. They begin to disperse when they are three months old and 5 millimeters (.2 inch) high.

Epiactis have colonized intertidal zones from Alaska to southern California. Assuming that they originated at the southern end and walked north, 2,500 kilometers (1,500 miles) seems a long distance to go, even in the twelve thousand years since the retreat of the last coastal glaciers. For this reason, ecologists often consider alternative mechanisms of transport, for instance hitchhiking on debris such as the holdfasts of uprooted and drifting kelp or sea grass. (Some forms of human-generated transport are considered in the last chapter as well.)

The small six-armed starfish *Leptasterias hexactis* (see Plate 94) also broods its young. Mature individuals are thought to congregate, with both sexes spawning more or less simultaneously. As the female liberates eggs, she collects into a cluster those that don't slip away, holding them with her tube feet and arching over them for six to eight weeks until the juvenile sea stars, approximately 2 millimeters (.1 inch) in diameter, are released. During that time, the brooding female cleans the egg mass, and because the position of the eggs blocks her mouth, she does not feed. While brooding, *Leptasterias* is more susceptible to being knocked off the substrate by waves because she holds on only with the tips of her arms. In rough water, she must allocate more of her tube feet to hanging onto the rock, decreasing the available brood area. In this way the rigors of the environment directly affect reproductive output.

With no planktonic dispersal stage, what accounts for the great geographic range of this species? It is found along the Pacific coast from Washington to California and is abundant on the Cobb Seamount, which lies 450 kilometers (270 miles) west of Washington State. Perhaps it is rafted from site to site by uprooted drifting kelp, such as *Nereocystis,* on which it sometimes crawls. At Cobb Seamount it also might be a persistent relic of times when sea level was 91 meters (300 feet) lower.

Plate 66

Plates 67 and 68 Snails and egg capsules

Mature individuals of the largely subtidal snail *Ceratostoma foliatum* sometimes gather in clusters in the intertidal zone to reproduce. After mating, females deposit eggs in fluted yellow teardrop capsules (Plate 67), which are attached to each other and to the rock. An adult female produces approximately forty egg capsules a year, each containing thirty to eighty eggs. Embryonic development, including metamorphosis, occurs within the capsule, and a miniaturized snail emerges in about four months.

The snail *Nucella canaliculata* breeds in spring and summer. After mating, the female deposits eggs in teardroplike capsules 6–11 millimeters (less than .5 inch) high, in clusters attached to the rocks in shaded situations (Plate 68). This species is one of several in which more eggs are laid in each egg capsule than actually develop; those that do not develop, called nurse eggs, are later eaten by the growing larvae to supplement their food supply.

Plate 67

Plate 68

Plate 69   Anemone asexual reproduction

Plate 70   Anemones shedding sperm

The sea anemone *Anthopleura elegantissima* is capable of two modes of reproduction, sexual and asexual. In Plate 69 it is seen reproducing asexually by
longitudinal fission, a process that takes about two days to complete. To some
extent it appears that fission is stimulated by starvation; a hungry anemone,
by dividing, tends to increase the size of its mouth relative to its metabolic
needs. In Plate 70, sperm are being shed into the water, while individuals
elsewhere shed ova. Fertilization takes place in the water when the eggs and
sperm meet. By relying on both modes of reproduction, the species is hedg-
ing its bets in an ecological as well as evolutionary sense. Fission permits a
genotype (clone) to occupy or monopolize space rapidly, potentially excluding
invaders. Sexual reproduction is favored for dispersal to new habitats, and it
also maintains genetic variability, an important way of adjusting to an unpredictable and changing world.

80

Plate 69

Plate 70

Plate 71   Nudibranch mating ritual

Plate 72   Nudibranchs and egg ribbons

Plate 73   Egg ribbon on hydroid stalk

Encounters between two individuals of the nudibranch *Phidiana crassicornis* (Plate 71) can be aggressive, but more often they occur for purposes of mating. Nudibranchs are hermaphrodites, with individuals capable of both making and fertilizing eggs. The mating pair cross-fertilizes each other, sometimes after an elaborate mating ritual, and then each lays its eggs encased in a soft, distinctively looped gelatinous matrix varying from species to species in size, shape, color, and number of embedded eggs. Eventually these disintegrate, and the larvae hatch and swim away. Plate 72 shows the wide egg ribbon of the nudibranch *Archidoris montereyensis,* and in Plate 73 the narrow coil of eggs of another nudibranch is attached to a hydroid stalk.

When reproduction involves direct physical contact, one risk is potential cannibalism. Many nudibranchs, including *Phidiana* (Plate 71), are generalized feeders that become reproductive at a relatively small size and engage in rituals that involve mouthing or biting one another. This behavior may lead to one of the two being eaten, particularly if it is much smaller. In this way some individuals of the population will indeed be better fed, and it can serve as an effective means of population control.

82

Plate 71

Plate 72

Plate 73

Plate 74   Mating crabs

Plate 74 shows two crabs, *Cancer productus,* mating, an activity that involves the male grasping and carrying the female around for several days before she molts, at which point the eggs are fertilized. The male will remain with his mate until after her new carapace has hardened enough for normal activity. The female carries the developing young under her abdomen, protecting them for some time. Eventually the eggs hatch and the larvae escape to become members of the plankton.

Plate 75   *Pisaster ochraceus* and the brown alga *Hedophyllum sessile*

Species like *Pisaster,* in which sexes are separate and which freely broadcast their gametes into the water column, benefit from close proximity during reproduction, since it greatly increases the probability of fertilization. Conversely, isolated individuals some distance from other members of their species, while increasing local diversity, may not contribute to a population's reproductive output.

84

Plate 74

Plate 75

Plate 76   Snail broadcasting eggs

In Plate 76 the snail *Calliostoma ligatum* (with a highly eroded shell) is releasing eggs. This is the most common mode of reproduction for intertidal invertebrates. The eggs are broadcast into the sea, where fertilization takes place. The fertilized eggs develop into a larval stage that drifts an unknown time and distance before settlement. Life for planktonic larvae is very hazardous: the longer the time spent in the plankton, the greater are the chances of the larvae dying before settlement. However, an extended planktonic interval also increases the possibilities of traveling greater distances and encountering higher-quality habitat. Herein lies a very subtle balance between risk and reward.

Plate 77   Barnacle settlement

Barnacles are representative of a large number of invertebrate species whose larvae spend two to three or more weeks in the plankton. These larvae, loaded with sensory devices, can closely discriminate and identify the substrate on which they are settling. The larvae of the small barnacles in Plate 77 have already made their choice, settled, and, in the process of metamorphosis, shed much of their larval equipment. Now, attached to the substrate, they have assumed the appearance of miniaturized adults. Note that the distribution of these small, brown *Chthamalus dalli* appears to be related to the texture of the rock on which they settled. Many of them occur in tiny cracks, suggesting that this microenvironment is especially favorable to survival. The biological question is whether they choose to settle in such places or whether their distribution reflects more general settlement, with higher survival rates occurring in the little cracks and furrows. A major cause of barnacle mortality is limpets, which, as they move around, dislodge small, recently metamorphosed barnacles. This phenomenon, referred to as bulldozing, affects small balanoid barnacles more than it does *Chthamalus*. Thus, one might expect balanoid barnacles to choose sites without limpets in which to settle and, in general, for early survivorship of all barnacles to be enhanced by textured surfaces.

Larval capacities for habitat discrimination are important, especially for sessile species, since the choice once made commits the individual to a particular spot for life. Individuals that make inappropriate decisions are not apt to survive to reproduce, which explains the need for such sophisticated abilities during the critical transition from planktonic to benthic life.

Plate 76

Plate 77

Plate 78   Sea urchin recruitment

Sea urchins are typical of a great many marine invertebrates: the adult is abundant and its ecology well known, while the early life-history events just after metamorphosis are almost unknown. Many larval urchins prefer to settle close to adults, where presumably they are protected under a canopy of calcareous spines. It is known that urchins can live a long time, and in many areas recruitment to the population by larvae is irregular, with large numbers of young recruiting only once or twice a decade. This unpredictable pattern underscores the many dangers of human exploitation. Not only is the adult reproductive stock being removed, but so is the source of settlement cues or protection for the larvae. Under these circumstances, the rate of recovery after exploitation has ceased is apt to be slowed. In Plate 78, juvenile *Strongylocentrotus purpuratus* and *S. fransiscanus,* probably one to two years old, have emerged from under a canopy composed of adult sea urchins. Purple sea urchins are a species in which size is not a good indicator of age, for individuals are capable of increasing and decreasing in size in response to environmental conditions. Size does influence reproductive capacity, though, as larger individuals have more gonad and can potentially leave more offspring. However, there are fascinating and biologically important limitations to this generalization. When species broadcast their gametes, these rapidly become diluted in moving seawater, and that in turn greatly diminishes the probability of successful fertilization. Organisms can increase this probability by forming breeding aggregations and coordinating their spawning. In this sense, isolated individuals, even though large, well fed, and maximally reproductive, may be denied entry into the reproductive sweepstakes. Effective production of fertilized gametes may well be best accomplished by smaller individuals living in dense aggregations.

88

Plate 78

5

The Role of Color

Bright colors contribute much of the magic of the intertidal realm and their possible meanings are intriguing. Pigments may be obtained through diet or manufactured metabolically, and their use by individuals in recognition, camouflage, or to warn off potential predators suggests an adaptive function. Frequently, though, the biological significance of these brilliant hues remains a mystery.

Light, particularly solar radiation, is the fundamental source of energy for the life-giving process of photosynthesis, and without light there would be no color. The watery environment itself changes some of the properties of light and vision as we know them. Because light is absorbed and scattered as it penetrates water, underwater vision can be compared to that on land in fog. In the ocean, beyond a certain depth the only light that remains is that of bioluminescent origin, light produced by organisms themselves from photophores or bacteria. It is in the uppermost zones of the marine environment, then, that brilliant colors, subtle hues, varied patterns, warning coloration, and camouflage are best developed. The extravagant use of color characteristic of the ocean's lighted zones, moreover, implies relatively good vision, as is true for some crabs and octopus, and there are birds and fish whose color vision is comparable to ours, which is the standard against which all others are compared.

However, color vision is postulated for only a few marine invertebrates, and color discrimination has been demonstrated for still fewer. In one experiment the hermit crab *Pagurus* was shown to discriminate between painted yellow and blue snail shells and shells colored different shades of gray. Most other inter-

tidal species at least have photoreceptors of one sort or another that can identify differences in light intensity, but we don't know whether such organisms
detect color or movement, whether they can form an image, and, if they can,
how they respond to such stimuli. And even though the octopus eye, for example, is capable of forming an image, its visual perception must be different from
ours. It is often difficult enough to understand what imagery lies in the mind
of a human "beholder"; the problems are greatly magnified when marine invertebrates are under consideration.

Many colors have no known biological significance. In some organisms they
are the result of deep colored tissue showing through other, more transparent
body parts; in other animals strong colors or patterns remain concealed within
opaque bodies or shells; and many vividly colored animals live in burrows from
which they rarely emerge. With both the level of visual acuity and the ability to
detect color in question for most intertidal organisms, the role of color has been
difficult to ascertain

Color is of enormous significance to organisms that are eaten by predators
relying on visual cues to locate and capture prey. Consequently, many of the examples of adaptive coloration illustrated here could also have been considered
in the chapter on predation, particularly as examples of prey defenses. As such,
color is usually not an interactive process among organisms themselves, but
rather the result of one such as predation.

To interpret the significance of color requires a broad understanding of an
organism's life style. For some animals there may be a protective advantage in
being as conspicuous as possible, perhaps to advertise some unpalatable or noxious quality. One wonders if the predators of invertebrates learn to associate color
with certain unpleasant attributes, such as inedibility or high risk, as has been
well documented for birds. Color may also help one individual recognize another of its own species and to choose mates; it is just possible that the varied
hues and patterns of hermit crabs are used in this fashion.

From our viewpoint the enormous range of marine plant colors is enigmatic.
All algae possess the green pigment chlorophyll essential for absorbing light
used in photosynthesis; however, they may derive their color from a mix of photosynthetic pigments, the proportions of which determine the color we see.
Sometimes masking or accessory pigments are present in sufficient quantity to
disguise the pigment determining the division to which the plant belongs. Thus,
some high intertidal red algae (division Rhodophyta) appear brown.

Organisms that blend into and are often indistinguishable from their back-
grounds are said to be *cryptic*. Crypsis may originate from behavior, genetic fac-

tors, or developmental processes, and requires the ability to select a matching background. It assumes the predator has a seeing eye capable of color vision or at least pattern discrimination. Other animals employ mimicry, essentially fooling the predator by resembling some other more distasteful or dangerous form.

Some animals, including abalones and top shells, gain their color as a result of diet, perhaps because pigments in their food aren't metabolized and are somehow transferred and laid down in their bodies or shells. Although this procedure may seem rather casual, it guarantees that an organism, eating what's around it, will inadvertently and generally match its background coloration. Many animals have color that is both fixed and beyond their control, but some of these also belong to a species that is polymorphic, existing in a number of color modes. Some animals acquire protective color passively or actively on their exterior surfaces, such as the deceiving collections that decorator crabs affix to their carapaces. Others are capable of modifying their color by use of chromatophores, pigment-containing cells that can be manipulated by the animal's musculature to produce color change in a flash.

When an organism stands out against its background, are we seeing a technique for self-advertising or a sign that it has wandered into foreign and potentially hostile habitat? What is the function of the bright and highly characteristic nudibranch colors? Why should the large barnacle *Balanus nubilus* have a sulphur-yellow mantle? Why should hydrocorals stuffed under rocks be purple, orange, or red? And why do sponge and starfish exhibit the colors they do? Many uses of color are represented in the photographs that follow, but examples also appear of intertidal color that we cannot explain with certainty regarding cause or functional significance. Thus, it is color—on both dainty and grotesque species found under rocks or in caves both high and low in the intertidal zone—with its pronounced influence on human visual sensations, that continues to intrigue biologists and many others, who wonder whether nature's striking and ornate displays are simply capricious or signify important biological interrelationships.

Plate 7 9   The sunflower starfish, *Pycnopodia helianthoides*

Plate 8 0   Top shells, *Calliostoma ligatum*

Plate 79

Plate 80

Plate 8 1   Iridescent algae

There are three groups of large benthic algae: reds, browns, and greens. Some of the red algae are iridescent: their color changes as one's angle of view does—a delightful phenomenon and one distinct from the biochemical production of colors from pigments. The phenomenon may have different causes in different algae. In the red alga *Mazzaella chordata* (Plate 81), iridescence is produced on the blade of the plant by an outer *cuticle,* a series of thin, laminated layers of cells spaced in such a way that the structure internally absorbs one wavelength of the spectrum's rays while reflecting the rest. This pattern produces contrasting indices of refraction, or iridescence. Oddly enough, the color of these plants may be incidental to one of the cuticle's functions—that is, protecting the plant's tissues from attacks by grazing amphipods.

Plate 8 2   Fleshy red algal crust, *Hildenbrandia* sp.

Plate 8 3   Intertidal flora

The saclike plant *Halosaccion glandiforme* (Plate 83), another red alga, can vary in color from yellow to dark red as the amount and color of the light striking the plant vary. In addition, some of the variation may be induced by the plant's reproductive state. Also seen in this photograph are a green alga, *Ulva* sp., and both crustose and erect forms of coralline algae, which are reds.

In addition to illustrating variations in plant color, Plate 83 hints at the range of morphological variety so characteristic of marine algae. *Ulva* is essentially a two-layered sheet of photosynthetic tissue. The sheet form, the most common morphology in the intertidal zone, presents a large surface area to the sun, thus maximizing photosynthetic area with minimal strain on the holdfast. The adaptive significance of the *Halosaccion* form, a balloon of tissue surrounding a cavity partially filled with sea water, has not been investigated. Perhaps the entrapped water helps keep the plant moist and cool by evaporative water loss when exposed on a hot day. Or—again, perhaps—the internal water holds the plant off the surface, making it more difficult for herbivores to eat.

The coralline algae all start out as discs closely adherent to the rock surface. Some never depart from this life form, though they do show wide variation in thickness, surface texture, and positioning of the reproductive structures;

94

Plate 81

Plate 82

Plate 83

these are referred to as crustose coralline algae. The other corallines similarly begin as a crustose basal system that eventually develops erect branches composed of many-jointed plates. The erect forms are as varied and taxonomically difficult as the crusts.

Plate 84   Detail of lower intertidal marine alga, *Desmarestia* sp.

Overlapping fronds on a flat surface suggest the potential for self-shading, which would reduce photosynthesis. These conditions are alleviated, however, when the plant is immersed and wafted about by water motion.

96

Plate 84

Plate 85   Intertidal algae

Plate 85 illustrates a number of species of algae. Particularly conspicuous is a species of brown algae, *Pelvetia fastigiata*. Its characteristic color comes from an accessory photosynthetic pigment that both protects the primary pigments and contributes to the plant's productivity. The mosslike *Cladophora* sp., a green alga, is also present.

Plate 86   A sea anemone, *Urticina* sp., and mobile organisms: a hermit crab, the snail *Calliostoma ligatum*, the sea urchin *Strongylocentrotus droebachiensis*, and the chiton *Katharina tunicata*

98

Plate 85

Plate 86

Plate 87   The floor of a surge channel with sea anemones and sponge. Note that all of the rock surface is inhabited.

Plate 88   Brittle star

The brittle star *Ophiopholus aculelata* is, like *Pisaster ochraceus,* an echinoderm that exhibits extremely varied hues and patterns for no known reason. The variations of the arms, moreover, are independent of the design of the central disc. No two *Ophiopholus* have been found to be exactly alike. In Plate 88, the narrow gap separating the sponges suggests both that they are different individuals and that sponges have self-recognition capabilities.

100

Plate 87

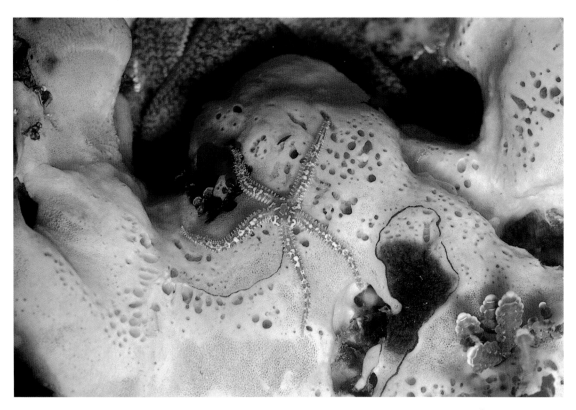

Plate 88

Plate 89 Nudibranch

Individual members of a species may exhibit a high degree of variation in color and pattern owing to a combination of genetic factors, the arrangement of pigments, and variations in diet. This is certainly true of *Phidiana crassicornis* (Plate 89); however, this nudibranch is always recognizable, even in juvenile stages, by the presence of a brilliant orange stripe down its back and bright blue lines along each side. In general, nudibranchs may be either cryptic or conspicuously colored. Nudibranchs such as *Phidiana* do have something noxious to advertise. Their diet is composed largely of coelenterates such as hydroids that possess nematocysts, minute stinging structures. These are swallowed whole, transported through the gut and across its lining unexploded, and eventually lodge in club-shaped or branching dorsal protuberances called ceratae, where they serve to defend the nudibranch. Some species wave their ceratae when disturbed. The striking bright coloration of this nudibranch is thought to be a warning to potential predators. How effectively it works and whether the predators learn to associate the nudibranch's color and pattern with inedibility isn't known.

Plate 90   The starfish *Pisaster ochraceus*

Many starfish are polymorphic in color, as is *Pisaster,* with individuals varying in hue from bright orange to a vivid purple. No reasons for this are known. Gulls that hunt visually are probably not involved, since large individual *Pisaster* cannot be considered camouflaged or cryptically colored. For whatever reason, the orange morph is more common along exposed shores and the purple is more abundant in calmer, more sheltered waters.

Two-toned individuals like this one are exceptionally rare. Is this individual recovering from a wound, or is this unique coloration the result of a developmental anomaly?

Plate 89

Plate 90

Plate 91   Nudibranch

In Plate 91, the nudibranch *Diaulula sandiegensis* is easy to spot. Its hard, gritty surface texture may contribute to discouraging predators, as might the prominent ring-shaped markings on its back, the number of which varies from individual to individual. For an organism without vision, such as this, the color displayed in ring shapes may function in two ways. Like the false eyes on butterflies, fish, and birds, the rings might appear to be large eyes and startle predators. Or the "eyes" may simply serve to break up an otherwise continuous surface color, thereby rendering the nudibranch more cryptic. If nudibranchs had excellent color vision we would have to consider another hypothesis: that the striking colors serve as sexual signals to prospective mates.

Plate 92   Cryptic isopod

Color and form together often make an animal difficult to detect or follow, as in the isopod *Idotea* sp., seen in the center of Plate 92. The isopod's exoskeleton, which is composed of overlapping plates, is well suited to blend with the articulated architecture of erect coralline algae. When the animal and plant share a common coloration, the crypsis is near perfect. One problem with this strategy is that the isopods are restricted to coralline algal turf, since when they leave it they become conspicuous prey items.

Another and less common form of protective coloration occurs when one animal species assumes the body form and coloration of another to gain protection. Such mimicry usually involves imitation of well-defended, aggressive, or inedible species.

Plate 93   Nudibranch, egg masses, and sponge

The cryptic nudibranch *Rostanga pulchra* and its egg masses are usually found on one of its preferred prey items, the red sponge *Ophlitaspongia pennata*. As the nudibranch feeds it incorporates pigments from the sponge. The eggs it lays in a transparent jelly matrix are also brightly colored, but as development proceeds they become paler.

104

Plate 91

Plate 92

Plate 93

Plate 94   Cryptic starfish

There are at least fifteen *Leptasterias* starfish in this picture, some of which are very hard to discern against a typically diverse and varied background. Mottled coloration may make this small starfish difficult for a potential predator—hunting by sight—to discover. Predators hunting by smell would have better luck. As predators themselves, starfish concentrated at high density in such a small space would have considerable impact ecologically.

Plate 95   The blood star, *Henricia* sp., perched atop two of its food items, the sponge *Halichondria panicea* and the bryozoan *Cryptosula* sp.

Plate 94

Plate 95

Plate 96 Lined chiton

Plate 96 features the small lined chiton *Tonicella lineata,* whose markings, sinuous or zigzag lines, resemble those of no other Pacific coast species. In contrast to *Leptasterias,* the color of *Tonicella* is known to be modified by diet. These mollusks are pinker when eating coralline algae and greenish when feasting on diatoms.

Plates 97 and 98 Cryptic coloration in fish

Oligocottus maculosus, a small sculpin, is expert at matching its background, such as the rock in Plate 97. This species is abundant on rocky shores, especially in tidepools. Another sculpin, *Clinocottus* sp., also demonstrates the ability to match its background, a sponge, in Plate 98. Animals such as octopus and some fishes can rapidly alter their color in relation to background color and light intensity by use of chromatophores, and they know when they have reached a good match. Such controlled use of color makes their predators' search more difficult. At the same time, it may serve to conceal the fish, as predator, from its prey.

Plate 96

Plate 97

Plate 98

Plate 99   Decorator crab

An interesting camouflage technique is seen in certain crabs. Because the crab exoskeleton is an armor composed of nonliving tissue, the adjustable color patterns characteristic of some fish and octopus aren't possible for these species. Crustaceans have used at least two techniques to counter this limitation. In the first, small-bodied crustaceans will match their background coloration (see Plate 92). The second solution is seen in larger-bodied species, which are bound to have greater food requirements and must move around more, so are unlikely to be adapted to some local color. This solution is illustrated by the spider crab *Oregonia gracilis,* which decorates itself with a veritable garden and/or bestiary on its back. In Plate 99, *Oregonia* is covered with a luxuriant growth of tunicates and sponges. This camouflage is actively acquired, transplanted, and maintained by the crab and must be replaced after each molt. It produces a generalized coloration, texture, and outline well suited to the crab's general feeding and habitat requirements. The rough texture of *Oregonia*'s carapace encourages settlement of various colonists, but the crab also has delicate pinchers on its first pair of legs that are well designed for handling and planting bits and pieces of plant and animal decoration. Other species become camouflaged passively and acquire an epibiota naturally, such as the limpet *Acmaea mitra* (see Plate 45). However, uncontrollable epibiont growth can be detrimental, making organisms more susceptible to being dislodged, as witnessed in many limpets, mussels, chitons, and even large algae found stranded along the beach after storms.

Plate 100   Solitary corals

Balanophyllia elegans is the only true coral occurring intertidally along the Pacific coast. It is most often found under ledges, in caves, and in other dark places. The brightly colored polyp is retractable into a stony, craterlike skeleton with radiating ridges, which appears bony and chalk white when the animal dies. Currently, there is no explanation for the distinctive color of this species.

Plate 99

Plate 100

Plate 101 Sea anemones

The color of the sea anemone *Anthopleura xanthogrammica* can be attributed in part to natural pigmentation, but mainly to symbiotic green algae. These become concentrated in the tissue lining the digestive tract, branches of which extend into the core of each tentacle. The value of the association is in part a nutritional one: organic compounds produced by the plants are utilized by the anemone, while algal endosymbionts use the anemone's carbon dioxide (CO_2) and nitrogenous wastes in photosynthesis. *A. xanthogrammica* is more fit with the algae than without, yet in areas of low light intensity where photosynthesis isn't possible, the anemone survives without the symbiont and is much paler in color.

Plate 102 Starfish color

The vividly colored starfish *Orthasterias koehleri* can be found low in the intertidal zone. It ranges from pink to bright red with markings in a variety of other colors. In general, starfish coloration remains a little-understood phenomenon. Many species, though brightly colored, have no known noxious qualities other than pedicellaria, or pinching organelles.

Plate 101

Plate 102

Plate 103   Goose barnacles, *Pollicipes polymerus*

These stalked barnacles are characterized by a striking pattern of small calcareous plates. Surprisingly, some color morphs of the limpet *Lottia digitalis* develop a shell patterning mimicking that of the barnacles' lateral plates.

Plate 103

6

Nature's Variability:

Understanding the Changing Patterns, Conserving the Species

The intertidal zone is in flux from day to day, month to month, and year to year. The variations in time and space that occur at every site may have slight effect, or they may all but drown out the major patterns. On rocky shores at temperate latitudes, the occasional bad storm, the equally devastating spell of cloudless sky and still, low water (which afflict the intertidal with a desert climate for six hours a day), or even a loose log kicked around by the waves can have a dramatic influence. Such events can kill large numbers of mussels, limpets, and other animals, and wipe out areas of kelp and benthic algae, thus providing opportunities for new settlers. Scientists, although unable to predict precisely when and where disturbances such as these will occur, have found them to be exceptionally revealing about how whole assemblages respond to extreme, infrequent events.

Some "disruptions" of normal intensity are cyclical, like the onset of winter. Every year, following the autumnal equinox, storms rip out sea palms and strip many other kelps of their fronds, so that a rocky shore, like a deciduous forest, can appear in midwinter to be a relatively lifeless place. Such rhythms are individual: each shore has its own, governed by the cycles of activity in its long-lived species and the seasonal timing of settlement, growth, reproduction, and death in its shorter-lived members. Some organisms, characterized by their hit-and-run behavior, seem attuned to take advantage of the opportunities opened by these seasonal disruptions. In midwinter, for example, the spores of *Porphyra* settle high on the shore and grow prolifically, splashed by the same winter storms that depopulate the rocks lower down. As spring comes and the water begins to warm, the newly exposed rocks often acquire a slippery coating of diatoms. Kelps begin to grow and, eventually, shade the diatoms, reducing their abundance. The opportunists cannot persist, despite temporary periods when they may blanket the intertidal, either because they are poor competitors or are good to eat.

Different sets of opportunistic species characterize the summer and fall. Because seasonality is their hallmark, they usually produce little change in the longer-term nature or appearance of the baseline community. The easiest way to recognize them—indeed, the only way without more precise biological information—is to visit a favorite site a number of times throughout the year and note the pulses of life.

Other marine disturbances are less predictable in space and time, much like their terrestrial counterparts: landslides, tornadoes, forest fires, deep footprints in soft mud, or the dirt mounds of moles and badgers. In the intertidal zone, a winter storm can open a gap in a mussel bed, or deep freezes can kill large expanses of kelp, even whole populations of certain organisms. These events remove organisms of one sort and in so doing either recycle some limiting resource or present a new resource favoring another and different assemblage.

Biologists are now beginning to understand that disturbance provides an important opportunity for diversity. Too much disturbance can became a monotonous stress with monotonous results, but a moderate frequency enlivens and enriches the environment by creating a mosaic of life, occupying patches of different ages and sizes.

The nature of the biological assemblage within the patches themselves changes with time. This phenomenon is generally referred to as *succession*—the pattern of species replacements following some large-scale disruptive event. A landslide-cleared forest, for instance, would be recolonized by a series of plants, each slower to arrive and longer-lived than the last, until (usually, but not always) the vegetation in that clearing was restored to its original composition. The same is generally true on rocky shores, except that the sessile colonists are both plant and animal. It is now known that the order in which the species arrive and the nature of their interactions may produce local variations in the replacement sequence. For this reason some early views on succession have been called into question, but no one would disagree that the post-disturbance species composition of a site changes with time.

On rocky shores we can identify two prevalent categories of physically caused natural disturbance, both leading to mortality and therefore to change. The first includes extreme physical and mechanical stresses, as in the destruction of mus-

117

sel beds by wave action or battering by logs. In these cases, individual survival depends not so much on superior attributes as on the good fortune of being out of harm's way when the disruption occurs. This type of disturbance can produce a patchy, heterogeneous population or even a collage of different species, and can be a major determinant in the overall pattern and character of a shore. It is also relatively easy to recognize: gaps in mussel beds, recently overturned boulders, sand scour marks on pier pilings or rocks, or rock surfaces that have exfoliated. None of these is likely to have been caused by the normal activities of organisms, and all are readily related to localized nonbiological processes.

The second source of mortality is more predictable, and occurs when the physiological limits of an organism are exceeded, for instance by heat, cold, or insufficient oxygen. These stresses usually come to bear at the extremes of vertical ranges, most commonly toward the upper limit, and result in a uniform pattern or band of death paralleling the water level over a broad geographic area. Careful observation can often reveal dead or moribund individuals above this limit. The activities of predators or competitors may also create sharp boundaries. Exceptionally stressful events, however, can eliminate whole populations. Visit your favorite shore immediately after a "hundred-year" storm or freezing spell: the destruction and death can be appalling.

It is important to recognize the distinction between the natural physical disturbances and stresses with which organisms have evolved for eons, and the newer, different challenges introduced by humans that can also influence natural communities adversely. Intertidal organisms that have adapted to the dynamic ebb and flow of natural disruptions may well suffer from additional human-induced stress. Because opportunistic or "weedy" organisms are apt to mature within a year or less, they are in a sense pre-adapted to an existence filled with vagaries. The individuals of many other species, on the other hand, take more than a year to mature sexually and may attain great age. These individuals cannot respond rapidly to environmental change. Once such species have been removed, they take years to return: giant sequoia trees recover more slowly from harvesting than dandelions. On marine shores, commercial exploitation of the red alga *Porphyra* seems feasible; the same has not proven true, in the absence of enforced regulations, for slow-growing, long-lived abalone, urchins, and giant kelp.

Perhaps the oldest form of human disturbance on the rocky shore is the harvest of edible species. A seafood market or restaurant menu presents a rich array of delicacies: abalone, urchins, barnacles, anemones, limpets, snails, and even alga, all harvested from the shore. In California, overharvesting has reduced

118

the subtidal white abalone population to less than 0.1 percent of its natural density. This species, as a result, is commercially extinct (it can no longer be harvested for profit, or even recreational enjoyment); it is probably ecologically extinct (it can at best minimally perform its ecological role in the food web), and may be approaching evolutionary extinction (in the absence of a massive restoration program, the white abalone will possibly disappear altogether). Abalone are not the only species at risk: more than half the world's fishery stocks are today considered fully or overly exploited. Overexploitation not only affects the harvested species but also cascades through the community to influence every connected species.

While overharvesting can reduce or eliminate a species in its community, the addition of new species to a community can be equally devastating. Natural communities have evolved in some degree of isolation from each other, separated by continental land masses and the vast expanses of oceans and diverging current systems. The rocky shores of the east and west coasts of North America, for example, hosted the evolution of largely unique native communities, with the continental land mass minimizing invertebrate and algal dispersal between them. While creatures have naturally walked, crawled, swum, and floated to extend their ranges over millions of years, humans have rapidly and efficiently introduced species across natural barriers into communities they would not have reached by themselves. Some of these introductions are intentional: Asian oysters grow side by side with Mediterranean mussels in shellfish farms around the world; Atlantic salmon and saltmarsh cordgrass were introduced to the Pacific Northwest for aquaculture and erosion control, respectively. With these intentional introductions, however, have come pesky hitchhikers, for instance the carnivorous gastropods successfully added to the Pacific coast fauna during failed attempts to establish Atlantic oysters.

Hitchhiking species also travel with maritime traffic along commercial shipping routes and through canals that unite previously isolated bodies of water. For centuries, wooden boats and ships moved slowly across the world's oceans, providing a free ride for animals and plants settled on the hulls. Today, steel-hulled ships coated with antifouling paint carry fewer adults on the outside, but more larvae on the inside. Every commercial vessel loads harbor water, teeming with fish and invertebrate larvae and algal spores, to provide ballast during the voyage. As ballast water is discharged, an international assemblage of living species is unceremoniously discarded into the waters of their new homes. Not every arrival survives, but those that do can change the community in ways both subtle and overwhelming. It is a deceptive notion that the flood of introductions leads to increased biodiversity, with its presumed ecological advantages. With changes possible at genetic, behavioral, population, community, and ecosystem levels, the potential for introduced species to wreak havoc with native species is tremendous. As each new introduction follows increasingly swiftly on the heels of the last, this global merger leads to a homogenization of communities and changes in diversity on a planetary scale.

One of the most interesting puzzles for marine biogeographers and taxonomists today is to sort out the history of those cosmopolitan species that are found in marine communities around the world, and to predict and understand the consequences of their introduction. Obviously, all species at some point in their history are biological newcomers. For those few species that occur now worldwide—for example, a sponge native to and common on our shores, *Halichondria panicea*—it is important to understand, if possible, when and how their successful invasions occurred. This will aid our understanding of the human-initiated, increasing pace of the invasions occurring now.

While the biological pollution of species introductions has only recently registered on the radar of political concern, chemical pollution has been featured in the media since Rachel Carson's eloquent tale of DDT damage in *Silent Spring*. In the marine realm, oil spills are among the highest-profile sources of chemical pollution. Although the *Exxon Valdez* oil spill of 1989 received vast media attention, it was only one of many such events, with thousands of tons of oil continuing to be spilled every year. A single spill from an oil platform or tanker releases a drifting slick that can coat many kilometers of shoreline and kill thousands of mammals, birds, invertebrates, and algae, through hypothermia, suffocation, or poisoning. The cleanup process is at best equivocal and at worst even more damaging than the initial spill, as birds and mammals die from the stress of capture and high-pressure hot water and detergent scour the rocky shore, killing intertidal plants and animals that might otherwise have recovered.

Oil spills cause what is called point source pollution, meaning it has an identifiable source. Much harder to identify and trace is nonpoint source pollution, from multiple, diffuse sources: for example, the sheen of oil trailed behind boats and ships or the pesticide and herbicide runoff from heavily treated urban lawns, golf courses, and agricultural fields. Even the essential nutrients required by all life can become too much of a good thing: when high concentrations of nutrients flood into coastal waters from fertilized lands, sewage, and aquaculture farms, they may jump-start the growth of tiny single-celled dinoflagellates. In sufficient numbers, these miniature algae become visible as red tides and can be the lethal agents of paralytic shellfish poisoning. Atmospheric change such as today's unprecedented anthropogenic alterations of global climate affects the oceans. As the water temperatures rise measurably, some species will migrate to remain within their thermal limits; others may adapt genetically to the new regime; and still others will probably become extinct.

Learning to recognize and interpret both natural and human-caused disturbances, some of which are illustrated in the accompanying photographs, provides insights vital to the understanding and management of our limited rocky shorelines. Visit, for example, an unpolluted, unexploited rocky shore that is exposed to moderate to heavy wave action. Evidence of small-scale disturbance will be widely present, even stark. The community will be rich in species, many of which are relatively large and long-lived, and much patterning will be visible. At less exposed sites, where the natural physical disturbance regime is milder, the same assemblage is apt to be simpler: fewer species will coexist and spatial patterning will be less obvious. Finally, examine a polluted or heavily exploited shore. It is a safe bet that this will be weed-dominated, with the longer-lived components absent. Under a normal regime of disturbance, opportunistic species enrich rocky shores. Where people have accelerated the natural disturbance pace through overexploitation or have poisoned the longer-lived, more susceptible species, the native community can be greatly reduced in richness and even approach the boring. These heavily disturbed communities also host more than their share of introduced species, which blurs the mosaic of native biodiversity.

We start this chapter by illustrating the seeming immutability of zonation patterns. However, this impression disguises the distinctive signatures of disturbance, both physical and biological: wave-generated patterns, those produced by organism-organism relationships, and the possible consequences of species introductions. We conclude by illustrating the challenge humanity faces—and our hope that ecological understanding, enhanced by esthetic appreciation, will help preserve these species-rich ecosystems for future generations.

121

Plate 104   Intertidal zonation

Many rocky shores are characterized by a series of horizontal bands, each
dominated by a different conspicuous species of plant or animal and separated from the others by more or less sharp boundaries. The delineations are
sharper in some places than others, and this can tell us something important
about the local conditions of life. One may find from two to as many as eight
clear bands, depending in part on the exposure of the site to wave action. That
these general features persist through time despite battering by storm waves
attests to effective attachment mechanisms (glues and fibers for barnacles
and mussels), streamlined profiles (limpets), and flexibility (fleshy algae).
However, this apparent consistency through time is an illusion, disguising
the vital dynamics and smaller-scale changes so characteristic of such shores.

   Plate 104 displays a complex zonation pattern often characteristic of wave-
exposed habitats. At the top is a dark band of blue-green bacteria, which is
followed sequentially by a band of the barnacle *Balanus glandula,* a brown-
colored band of the red alga *Endocladia muricata,* a fringe of the small blue
mussel *Mytilus trossulus* (formerly *M. edulis*), a band of the larger *M. californianus,* a mixed band of the goose barnacle *Pollicipes polymerus* and the acorn
barnacle *Semibalanus cariosus,* followed by a zone inhabited by laminarian
algae and a great variety of lower intertidal invertebrates such as sponges,
tunicates, and sea urchins. This photograph is from 1981, but pictures of the
same shore taken in 1936 and 1998, not shown here, are essentially identical.
At this temporal scale, consistency is the rule, and change is not apparent.

122

Plate 104

Plate 105   A surge channel, with mussels and sea palms, in 1983

Plate 106   The same site in 1998

The sea palm, *Postelsia palmaeformis*, seen in Plate 105 as a miniature forest on our side of a surge channel, is an annual species, appearing in this phase of its life cycle from six to nine months. Such species are notoriously variable in space and time. Thus, in the fifteen years separating the photographs, although mussels and acorn and goose barnacles, all relatively long-lived species, remain conspicuous members of the assemblage, *Postelsia* has virtually disappeared.

Such variability provides both the excitement of discovery and the disappointment of failing to find some expected or favored species during intertidal exploration. It can also be the bane of ecologists: do radical changes in some species' distribution and abundance portend important shifts in a regional environment or simply reflect natural variation? Distinguishing between the two is fundamentally important to management decisions in a world threatened by global climate change.

124

Plate 105

Plate 106

Plate 107   Tidepool, 1980

Plate 108   Tidepool, 1981

Plates 107 and 108, of the floor of the same lower intertidal pool, were taken
one year apart. A quick glance at the color difference is enough to reveal the
dynamic nature of these assemblages. Some species have been partly eaten,
others have moved in or left completely, and others have changed position
slightly. The sea anemones, although long-lived and capable of relocating
themselves, don't seem to have moved. The red sponge, *Ophlitaspongia* sp.,
has persisted in almost the same place, whereas another sessile sponge, the
yellow *Mycale* sp., has disappeared; perhaps it was eaten or died of old age.
In the 1981 picture two mobile consumers, a small six-armed starfish, *Leptasterias hexactis,* and the keyhole limpet, *Diodora aspera,* are on the scene.
Diodora, which eats sponges, may have eaten the *Mycale.*

126

Most intertidal landscapes are so complex, and the changes so subtle, that
time-lapse photography at intervals of days to a year is essential if the dynamics are to be recorded adequately. More frequent photographs, of course, will
be more revealing and can help to remove some of the uncertainty surrounding the inevitability of biological change.

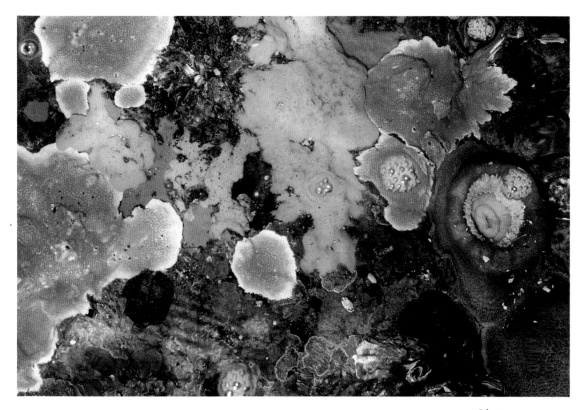

Plate 107

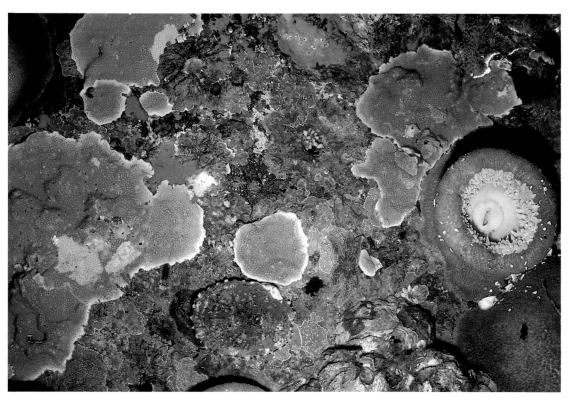

Plate 108

Plate 109   Waves sweeping over a mussel bed

Water motion brings both good news and bad news. Moving water delivers nourishment and larvae while removing metabolic wastes and inhibiting predators. At sufficiently great velocities, however, it can carve out large patches or destroy whole beds.

Plate 109

Plates 110 and 111   Gaps in mussel beds

Physical disturbance is particularly conspicuous when it affects species such as the mussel *Mytilus californianus*. Because it is competitively superior, this species is able to form expansive beds, or monocultures. Plate 110 shows a mussel bed with gaps where mussels were swept away. One gap is new (foreground), where the rock is mostly bare except for remnants of byssal threads and large old barnacles, *Semibalanus cariosus,* which have survived beneath the mussels for an unknown period of time. The adjacent gap is older, having formed during the previous winter, and is now thoroughly saturated with small *S. cariosus* and assorted algae. Plate 111 shows another mussel bed, similarly disrupted. The foreground gap here contains a distinctive set of organisms, predominantly the benthic green alga *Ulva* sp. and some red alga, *Halosaccion glandiforme.* Two other gaps are visible in the background: a recently formed one characterized by ample bare rock, and a slightly older one carpeted by green algae. All will eventually revert to mussels.

Scientists are as uncertain why some patches are initially small and others large as they are about the exact mechanisms of patch formation. Predators, floating logs, or the lifting and shearing forces of large waves could all initiate such disturbances. Once cleared, the patches may continue to expand as wave action further unravels the edges of the surrounding mussel bed. Eventually, however, expansion ceases and patches are closed, either as mussels encroach inward from the perimeter or by the settlement of new mussels. Natural disturbances provide space where other organisms can grow during the time it takes the mussels to return, and in many instances this valuable spatial resource is snapped up on a first come, first served basis. The time of year the gap is opened, its height in the intertidal zone, and its size when formed all affect the further characteristics of the patch, its recolonization, and the subsequent succession of organisms that occupy it.

130

Plate 110

Plate 111

Plate 112   A sea urchin barrens

Plate 113   The California sea otter (photo © Norbert Wu)

Sea urchins are long-lived invertebrates, and when they exist at high density, their concentrations restrict the development of a kelp assemblage. Plate 112, featuring intertidal purple urchins, *Strongylocentrotus purpuratus,* illustrates some of the effects: no fleshy algae coexist with these urchins, and the small haloes seen around many of the urchins show that they have fed on the adjacent dark diatoms. Similarly, the black chiton, *Katharina tunicata,* has grazed away a patch of diatoms. The sea urchins probably produced the depressions in which they are sitting by scraping with their teeth and perhaps their spines. Plate 43 also illustrates a typical intertidal urchin barrens.

The relationship between urchins and sea otters (Plate 113) has produced a classic example of ecological interactions and their complexity. In the nineteenth century otters were hunted to near extinction throughout an enormous geographic range from Japan through the Aleutian Islands, British Columbia, and south to Baja California. Because sea urchins are generally their favored prey, inter- and subtidal urchins must have been plentiful during those times when otters were absent, and scenes like those shown in Plates 43 and 112 were probably commonplace. Effective otter conservation began with an international treaty in 1918, and their populations have expanded since, through both natural recolonization and purposeful transplants by state and federal agencies. And where the otters have flourished, intertidal urchin barrens have disappeared, thus altering the ecological and visual landscape.

Because ecologists have been able to study areas with and without otters, there is now a deep appreciation for their ecological impact. Where otters are abundant, kelp tends to flourish; where otters are absent, sea urchin—produced barrens are a commonly observed feature. But otters consume many other species, including pismo clams and abalones in California, and crabs, mussels, and urchins everywhere. In many ways they compete with people for marine resources, often very effectively. The management and conservation dilemma becomes acute when thriving otters threaten the very existence of other species, for example, some abalones in California. We will never know whether, in the past, some balance existed among otters, urchins, and algae. Otters are native to our west coast marine ecosystems and contribute to both their variety and variation. At high, perhaps historically unrealistic densities, they can also contribute to their degradation: therein lies the challenge for management and conservation.

132

Plate 112

Plate 113

Plate 114   A bat star

The distribution of every species on the rocky shore is determined by a combination of the organism's physiological tolerances, its dispersal ability, and the prey, competitors, and predators it encounters. Range extensions occur when a species disperses naturally, often with winds or currents, beyond its usual distributional limits to colonize a new location. Such range extensions may be precipitated by fluctuations in ocean circulation patterns or by shifts in temperature regime caused by glaciation cycles or global climate change. When a species moves to a new location under human agency, we witness the introduction of a nonnative species to a new community.

The bat star, *Asterina* (formally *Patiria*) *miniata,* is native to and common in California, where it is unusual among sea stars in consuming plant as well as animal matter. Extremely rare in Oregon and Washington, it appears again abundantly in British Columbia along the outer coast of Vancouver Island. At some point, apparently, the bat star extended its range northward from California to reach British Columbia, skipping the hundreds of kilometers in between. It is unknown what factors limit its abundance, even presence, in Washington and Oregon.

Plate 115   Impact of an invasion—a deformed and domed abalone infested with an introduced sabellid polychaete

The introduction of nonnative species amounts to biological pollution of native genes, species, communities, and ecosystems. Every species introduction surely has some impact on its new community; impacts run the gamut from the barely measurable to the ecologically and economically destructive.

The native red abalone is the basis of a large-scale, economically valuable shellfish farming industry on the Pacific coast of North America. This industry has suffered from the accidental introduction of a nonnative sabellid (fan worm) that hitchhiked with abalone shipments from South Africa to California. Through subsequent shellfish transfers, this pest has spread along the Pacific coast to farms from Mexico to Oregon. The tiny sabellid does not kill the abalone directly but interferes with the host's shell growth. Juvenile worms settle at the edge of the abalone shell, causing the host to interrupt its normal growth and manufacture a nacreous shell layer, resembling mother of pearl, over the worm. As this layer hardens, it does not kill the worm: it simply creates a sturdy home for the parasite, which grows to reproduce and incubate more larvae. If the sabellid infestation is heavy, the abalone stops

Plate 114

Plate 115

growing normally altogether; instead it repeatedly makes shell layers stacked vertically on each new crop of worms and eventually may occlude its own respiratory pores. These domed, stunted abalone never reach market size, and their shells, riddled with fan worm tubes, grow weak and brittle. Like most species introductions, the sabellid plague is difficult and expensive to eradicate; if it spreads into wild populations of other bivalves and snails, it may be impossible to control.

Plate 116   An adult common murre incubates its single egg while a chick waits nearby

Plate 117   An oiled and dying murre

Threats to the health and future of the shore are increasing at an alarming rate. The disfigurement shown in Plate 117 is tantamount to vandalism in the largest sense and should alert us to the dangers of chemical and biological pollution. Toxic waste dumping, oil spills, and the harmful detergents used to clean them up alter and may irrevocably destroy marine life.

Murres (*Uria aalge*) are a common Pacific coast seabird, typically nesting in cliff colonies and fishing offshore in enormous rafts of hundreds of swimming birds. A healthy murre is well insulated in the cold waters of the Pacific by the air trapped below its feathers. A murre coated with oil loses its precious insulation and succumbs to a combination of acute toxicity and hypothermia. The difficulty of assessing mortality and gauging recovery, even in a discrete event such as an oil spill, plagues the efforts of biologists, policy makers, and lawyers alike.

Some anthropogenic disturbances are obvious, but others such as global climate change are much more subtle and therefore easy to misinterpret. From the standpoint of regulation or preservation the problem is enormous, for individual species often reside in different habitats according to their life history phase, or depend on nutrients generated many leagues away. Moreover, most species are vulnerable to inimical influences produced beyond national boundaries and transported shoreward by the vagaries of currents. To date, no solution to such broad environmental problems has been found, and the challenge of stewardship has not been met. Appendix A offers a brief intertidal "etiquette," or ethic. Anything one does, even on the most local scale, to minimize the inadvertent effects of a journey into the intertidal zone will help preserve the seashore in its natural state.

136

Plate 116

Plate 117

Plate 118   A child discovers a rocky shore

Species are adapted to the erratic rhythm of natural disturbance. Can they accommodate the accelerating tempo of human assault? The greatest threats to marine systems today are overharvesting, introduced species, habitat loss, chemical pollution, and global climate change. The maintenance of our seashore heritage in the face of this onslaught depends on careful management. Effective regulation of harvested resources will reduce the risk of overexploitation. Establishing marine protected areas, with limited human access and activity, will help preserve relatively pristine habitats and their resident species. Individual species introductions are expensive, if not impossible, to eradicate; as one invasion piles in upon the next, the problem rapidly becomes insurmountable. The flood of invasions is better controlled by turning off the tap than by mopping up the mess. Measures to reduce, reuse, and recycle both chemical wastes and everyday materials will ameliorate some of the pollution and dumping pressures on marine habitats.

In her adult years, what might the pictured child find on the shore? Incorporating an environmental ethic now into our local and global activities could provide protection for the species of today and hope for the stewards of the future.

Plate 119   Wave action

Plate 118

Plate 119

Appendix A: Planning Your Visit to the Tidepools

TIDE TABLES

Tide tables for the west coast of North America are available in the newspaper, at boat marinas and fishing supply stores, or directly from the National Oceanic and Atmospheric Administration (U.S. Department of Commerce). These tables give daily predictions of the times and heights of high and low water for each day of the year at a number of places, designated as reference stations. Usually tidal differences are given too, from which one can calculate the approximate times and heights of the tide at many other sites (tide tables also contain the times of rise and set for both the sun and the moon). For anyone interested in knowing more about what generates tides, we suggest the explanation offered in Thomas Carefoot's book *Pacific Seashores* (see the reading list at the end of this book).

Each month there are two series of good low tides, which are associated with the new and full moon. On the Pacific coast, the series with the lowest tides generally occurs during the early to late mornings of the spring and summer. During fall and winter, the low tides occur later in the day and often fall after dark.

The accompanying sample tide table is for two North American sites on Friday, June 22, 2001. Here for San Francisco the highest tide, 2.0 meters (6.7 feet), occurs at 0000 (midnight), and the lowest tide, −.5 meter (−1.7 feet), at 0655 (6:55 A.M.). If you want to know the predictions for Point Reyes, California, look at the listing of tidal differences based on the datum for San Francisco. It will

San Francisco (Golden Gate Bridge), California June 2001				Pacific Beaches, Washington June 2001			
Day	Time	Ht./ft.	Ht./m	Day	Time	Ht./ft.	Ht./m
22	0000	6.7	2.0	22	0057	9.4	2.9
Fri.	0655	–1.7	–0.5	Fri.	0815	–1.8	–0.5
	1421	4.8	1.5		1448	7.3	2.2
	1840	2.8	0.9		2002	2.7	0.8

tell you to subtract 26 minutes from the predicted time of low water, making the low tide at 6:29 A.M., and that there is no difference to be applied to the height of low water. For another site the difference might be as much as an hour and a half later than that predicted for San Francisco. Be sure to note these local differences in tide predictions; there's nothing more frustrating than getting to the shore two hours after the tide has turned, only to watch a prime area disappear under the water.

On the west coast of the United States, the tidal height of 0.0 is the mean of the lower of the two low waters of each day averaged over many years. What this means for intertidalgoers is that any tide of 0.0 or slightly lower (indicated by a minus sign) will fleetingly expose all the upper and middle intertidal and some of the lower zones. A –1.0-foot tide will go out a little farther, and the exceptionally low –2.0-foot tides will expose even more of the intertidal zone. As a check of the tables will reveal, in the course of a year there may be relatively few such superb opportunities (low tides of –1.5 to –2.0) to explore the intertidal zone. A little planning will be richly rewarded.

SOME THOUGHTS ABOUT SAFETY

Whenever you make an excursion to the intertidal zone, always learn the predicted times and heights for high and low water, keeping in mind that these predictions of sea level can be affected by numerous factors such as wind, swells, and barometric pressure—conditions that can vary dramatically from site to site and day to day.

At any given locale and on any particular tide, it is prudent to study the nature of the water conditions and the lay of the land, and to note where waves are breaking and washing. Certain organisms, by nature of their habitat requirements, will tell you something about specific conditions around you. For instance, the presence of the sea palm, *Postelsia palmaeformis*, indicates that the area is subject to heavy surf. Before actually venturing into the intertidal zone, it is also advisable that you study the area and determine a "safe" spot or an escape route should an unexpectedly large wave roll in. If you are ever caught by an unexpected wave, try not to panic, and don't run. Lie down, if possible behind an embankment of some sort, hang on, and let the water rush over you.

While in the intertidal zone keep an ear tuned at all times for significant changes in the ocean's roar. Periodically check your watch and the tidal height so that the rising tide won't strand you by cutting you off from a safe route back to shore.

Wear foot gear that will provide good traction and keep you relatively dry. For comfort's sake, a pair of wool gloves (the fisherman's fingertipless type) will keep you warm and help prevent "barnacle bites"—the endless scrapes and scratches that result from negotiating barnacle-covered rocks. Be prepared to get sprayed occasionally by splash from rogue waves.

Within the limits of common sense, however, don't hesitate to explore. And have a good time!

INTERTIDAL ETIQUETTE

We can partake of the shore's delicate beauty without offending, overpowering, or destroying it, but to respect this habitat we do have to monitor our conduct. Visits to the intertidal zone require great sensitivity to the resident plants and animals.

How can we minimize the adverse effects of looking at organisms, handling them, taking them away to eat, or simply walking about among them? To begin with, just getting around the intertidal poses its share of problems.

Try to step on bare rock when possible, remembering that it can be slippery when covered with a thin film of diatoms or crustose algae. In the middle intertidal zone, where fleshy algae make the surface treacherously slippery, the acorn barnacles and mussels make much better footing. One can hardly avoid walking on them, but do tread as lightly as possible. These easily crushed animals are important to the economy of the shore, for they are major prey for a large number of invertebrate predators and they provide settlement sites for algae as well. Even the empty valves serve as refuge sites for small organisms, such as littorines, amphipods, and sundry worms. Walking on mussels may weaken

143

their structural continuity and make them more vulnerable to the shearing forces of waves. In the lowest intertidal, sea urchins that have been trampled often suffer broken spines and must devote energy to repairing the damage rather than to other essentials of urchin life such as growth or reproduction.

Piles of dead or dying organisms stranded above the high water line are often the blatant signs of human disturbance. If you do exercise your curiosity by handling animals, replace them in their natural habitat. Some animals are easily damaged by being picked up. For instance, if you attempt to pry a starfish from the rocks, some of its tube feet or occasionally an arm may break, increasing the eventuality that the animal will be dislodged or destroyed by wave action. Sea urchins need their tube feet as well, for if their ability to hold on to the rock is diminished, they may be washed into the mouths of large sea anemones.

Even the simple act of replacing certain organisms requires some concern and common sense. Place starfish in deep tidepools where gulls can't extract them. A haphazard toss of a crab or chiton may result in well-fed anemones. Take care to place the animals upright and on acceptable habitat. This is especially true for limpets and chitons, which cannot right themselves easily and cannot attach to most algae. For them, rock is better.

Nearly all animals are endangered by being removed from where they belong. Use care in turning over rocks to see what lives under them, and return the rocks to their original positions afterward, since the animals you find under such rocks or seaweed are probably there for a reason. Perhaps they can't withstand periods of desiccation, or perhaps by being underneath things they achieve some measure of protection from predators. Don't destroy their habitats.

Copies of state laws governing the harvesting and collecting of marine organisms are available at offices of the Department of Fish and Game. If you are planning to do any collecting, you should familiarize yourself with these regulations and be sure to avoid those areas where collecting is prohibited. If you are considering eating certain shellfish, such as clams or mussels, be sure to check for warnings of paralytic shellfish poisoning. At certain times during the year, organisms such as these concentrate a toxin produced by the plankton they eat, and ingesting "hot" clams or mussels can be fatal for humans.

The harvesting of mussels can accelerate disruption of the mussel bed and will produce habitat alterations just as clearcutting a forest does. Harvesters take only one species purposefully but may have drastic effects on a wide variety of others. Such examples are reasonably common and suggest a ripple effect of some magnitude, especially when the larger organism being exploited or damaged provides the more specialized habitats required by many others.

Sea urchin gonads are a delicacy to some palates. Urchins, like the starfish *Pisaster ochraceus,* play a particularly important role in the organization of our rocky shores, and substantial reductions in their local abundance produce wide-sweeping changes in the intertidal landscape—for instance, the unrestricted spread of mussels and kelps. Visitors to the shore must be sensitive to these possibilities.

The young of some organisms, such as starfish, sea urchins, and sea anemones, recruit only every few years; others, such as the edible sea palm, whose young almost never grow more than 1.5 meters (5 feet) from their parents, disperse poorly. Still others, such as the larvae of our largest sea urchin, *Strongylocentrotus franciscanus,* preferentially (and maybe exclusively) are attracted to adult individuals, where they find shelter under a forest of spines. Larvae of our goose barnacle, *Pollicipes polymerus,* sometimes recruit to patches of bare rock, but also to stalks of adult individuals. Organisms such as these, which don't recruit regularly, which recruit to established individuals of their own kind, or which are poor dispersers, will be slow to recover if removed. What would our shores be like without them?

The well-intentioned release of aquarium or grocery store organisms like lobsters and fish—or the seaweeds in which they are packaged—can wreak havoc with the genetics and ecology of native intertidal organisms. Fish, shellfish, and seaweed from a market or pet store should never be cast on a beach or deposited in a tidepool, for it does no favor to the resident, native organisms. Similarly, moving animals or plants across natural barriers from one area to another, either by hand or on boat hulls and trailers, can lead to unwanted species introductions. Carefully rinsing off boats and trailers between launches helps get rid of these hitchhikers and reduces the risk of causing a biological invasion.

Intertidal etiquette can travel home from the coast, too. Activities far from the shore can, surprisingly, still have an impact on intertidal species. The oil and soap washed off neighborhood cars on a summer morning may drain directly to the coast, affecting the life there. Most established car washes have facilities for collecting and cleaning rinse water before drainage. Similarly, pesticides and herbicides may make for postcard gardens and golf courses, as well as impeccable produce, but can damage or kill organisms living downstream. Enrichment from fertilizers applied to agricultural fields can cause unwanted and excessive nutrients in local waters. Even fertilizer can be too much of a good thing, causing eutrophication of local waters and leading to blooms of toxic algae. Supporting organic farms, developing biocontrol with native species, and learning to live with the occasional lawn dandelion will all help reduce the chemical and biological pollution of our shores.

Preservation, however, should include all species regardless of size and regardless of whether they play a particular known role. Thus, while scientific debate rages on the economic and ecological benefits of conservation, a parallel argument could be built on esthetic principles alone. A deep satisfaction comes of seeing, understanding, and caring for the natural world.

Appendix B: Classifying Animals and Plants

ANIMAL PHYLA

The following synopses list a few major features that determine why an animal belongs to a particular phylum and, on occasion, some features useful for distinguishing animals in the field. We have omitted animal groups that aren't commonly found in the intertidal zone. At a glance, some groups are very confusing—for example, there are tunicates that look like sponges, erect bryozoa that are difficult to distinguish from hydroids, small limpets that may mimic barnacles, and a bryozoan that looks like a tunicate. Needless to say, brief summaries like these are fraught with the problems of oversimplification and may not be adequate for making such distinctions. For anyone interested in knowing more about these animal groups, we suggest *Intertidal Invertebrates of California* by Morris, Abbott, and Haderlie, and E. N. Kozloff's *Seashore Life of the Northern Pacific Coast.*

Phylum Porifera: Sponges These consist of cells, many not even in definite layers, organized around a system of pores, canals, and chambers through which water is moved. There are no body organs, but the sponge is supported by a skeleton of spicules and fibers. The texture is often feltlike or gritty, and one or more openings from which water currents flow are visible. Sponges may be encrusting or vaselike in form.

Phylum Cnidaria: Jellyfish, Sea Anemones, Hydroids, and Cup Corals In these animals the body wall consists of two cellular layers, with the gut being the only cavity. There is no anus, and the single opening, the mouth, is surrounded by tentacles. These animals are radially symmetrical—that is, in cross-section they look like a wagon wheel.

Phylum Platyhelminthes: Flatworms   These bodies have three layers of cells and bilateral symmetry. Intertidal members are usually flat and broad. All are carnivorous, and pigmented eye spots are visible in the larger flat worms.

Phylum Nemertea: Ribbon Worms   These are slender, usually slightly flattened, and highly elastic in length. Many are very colorful. They possess a complete digestive tract with a mouth at one end and an anus at the other, as do all the groups discussed from this point on. They also have a circulatory system. A unique feature is their proboscis (an extensile organ), which is used to capture prey. When extruded, it often looks as though another worm is being disgorged.

Phylum Annelida: Segmented Worms   The most characteristic feature is the segmentation of the body, usually with groups of bristles associated with the segments. These worms also have a circulatory system, complete digestive tract, and—a feature not seen in earlier groups—a body cavity, or coelom, a fluid-filled space between the digestive tract and outer body wall.

Phylum Mollusca: Snails, Limpets, Chitons, Squid, Clams, Octopus, and Mussels   These animals have a body plan divided into head, muscular foot, and visceral mass that is covered by a mantle, which in most species secretes a shell and shelters the gills. The shell may be one unit, two hinged together, or eight shells in a row. Their organ systems are well developed, and in some of these animals, like the octopus, the sensory capacities are extraordinary. Because the molluscan shell fossilizes quite readily, the fossil record for this group is rich and extends back over 500 million years.

Phylum Arthropoda: Crabs, Hermit Crabs, Isopods, Amphipods, Acorn Barnacles, Sea Spiders, Goose Barnacles, Shrimp (and Insects and Spiders)   This is the largest of all phyla and shows enormous diversity. The animals tend to be divided into well-marked sections often grouped together in functional regions: head, thorax, and abdomen. They have a hard, chitinous exoskeleton and jointed appendages. Sensory organs, especially antennae and eyes, are well developed.

Phylum Bryozoa: Lace or Moss Animals   These animals always live attached to something and have a shingled or imbricated surface. They form colonies in many configurations of essentially separate microscopic individuals with a chitinous or calcareous skeleton. The animals have a lophophore—a U-shaped feeding structure that is a ring of tentacles surrounding the mouth.

Phylum Echinodermata: Starfish, Brittle Stars, Sea Urchins, and Sea Cucumbers   These animals are radially symmetrical, often pentamerous (five-rayed), with protruding calcareous skeletal structures, mobile tube feet operated by a water-vascular system, a complex digestive system, and a nervous system.

Phylum Chordata: Tunicates and the Familiar Backboned Types such as Fishes, Birds, Mammals, Reptiles, and Amphibians   These all have a notochord, dorsal nerve cord, and gills or gill slits; however, vertebrates lose some of these chordate characteristics as embryos, and tunicates have them in the larval stage only. All tunicates are sessile, growing singly, in clumps of several individuals, or as colonial masses in various shapes. Each individual has an incurrent and excurrent opening; both are often visible. The texture is usually firm with a slick surface.

PLANT DIVISIONS

It is difficult to trace precisely the origin and evolutionary relationships of the algae. They are classified according to pigmentation, general structure, food-storage products, and reproductive patterns, and the following paragraphs list some major features of the plant divisions represented in the intertidal zone. All algae use the green pigment—chlorophyll—for photosynthesis. The color of an alga, however, is usually due to accessory pigments that mask the green color.

Division Cyanophyta   These blue-green algae, or cyanobacteria, are inconspicuous but important in marine waters. They are most obvious above the high tide line of cliffs and rock walls in areas where there is some seepage. They are very simple organisms in terms of the structure of their cells (they lack chloroplasts and nuclei) and are believed to be ancestral to all other algae. Their color is variable, but they all have the blue (phycocyanin) and red (phycoerythrin) pigments.

Division Chlorophyta   Green algae are believed to be the ancestral stock from which land plants were derived. The group consists mostly of one-celled species, long filaments made up of chains of single cells, broad

149

flat sheets, and thick growths composed of many fine filaments woven together. They lack accessory pigments and thus they are usually green in color.

Division Bacillariophyta   Diatoms are one-celled plants that sometimes form filamentous colonies and that may have cell walls composed of silica. They store food as oil droplets within themselves. They occur in vast, uncountable numbers and are eaten by almost everything in the sea either directly or indirectly. They contain brown (phaeophytin) pigment, which gives them a golden brown color.

Division Phaeophyta   Brown algae possess fucoxanthin, a brown pigment. They are morphologically the most varied division, existing as filaments, stalks with blades, hollow sacs, and in the shape of cushions, to name a few plant forms. They also attain the largest body size of any group, with kelps exceeding 91 meters (300 feet) in length. Two unique features of this group are the kelp holdfasts (home for many organisms) and the float bladders, some of which contain carbon monoxide gas.

Division Rhodophyta   These are the red algae, characterized by the pigment phycoerythrin and a variety of other pigments. Hence, their colors vary. There are many plant shapes and styles of organization within the phylum: simple or finely branched filaments, broad sheets, and crusts with variable texture, toughness, and rigidity. They are the most advanced of the algal groups in terms of their reproductive structures and are notorious for their taxonomic difficulty.

The first list below provides references to general books on marine biology and ecology, natural historical details of intertidal plants and animals, and the taxonomy of Pacific coast organisms. The second list contains more technical books and the scientific literature relevant to the patterns and processes described. These numbered references are followed by a third listing that groups them by plate number. By no means are these references exhaustive; nor do they necessarily include references to the initial research. Rather, for the reader interested in pursuing these subjects further, they provide documentation of the phenomena discussed and an introduction to the scientific literature.

I

1.   Abbott, I. A., and C. J. Hollenberg. *Marine Algae of California*. Stanford: Stanford University Press, 1976.

2.   Branch, G., and M. Branch. *The Living Shores of Southern Africa*. Cape Town, South Africa: Struik, 1981.

3.   Brusca, G. J., and R. C. Brusca. *A Naturalist's Seashore Guide—Common Marine Life of the Northern California Coast and Adjacent Shores*. Eureka, CA: Mad River Press, 1978.

4.   Carefoot, T. H. *Pacific Seashores: A Guide to Intertidal Ecology*. Vancouver: Douglas; Seattle: University of Washington Press, 1977.

5.   Hedgpeth, J. W. *Introduction to Seashore Life of the San Francisco Bay Re-*

gion and the Coast of Northern California. California Natural History Guides, 9. Berkeley and Los Angeles: University of California Press, 1962.

6.   Kozloff, E. N. *Seashore Life of the Northern Pacific Coast.* (Rev. ed. of *Seashore Life of Puget Sound, the Strait of Georgia, and the San Juan Archipelago,* 1973.) Seattle: University of Washington Press, 1983.

7.   Kozloff, E. N. *Marine Invertebrates of the Pacific Northwest.* Seattle: University of Washington Press, 1987.

8.   Lewis, J. R. *The Ecology of Rocky Shores.* London: English University Press, 1964.

9.   Morris, R. H., D. P. Abbott, and E. C. Haderlie (with 31 text contributors). *Intertidal Invertebrates of California.* Stanford: Stanford University Press, 1980.

10.   O'Clair, R. M., and C. E. O'Clair. *Southeast Alaska's Rocky Shores.* Auke Bay, AK: Plant Press, 1998.

11.   Portmann, A. *Animal Camouflage.* Ann Arbor: University of Michigan Press, 1959.

12.   Ricketts, E. F., J. Calvin, and J. W. Hedgpeth. 5th ed., rev. D. W. Phillips. *Between Pacific Tides.* Stanford: Stanford University Press, 1985.

13.   Smith, R. I., and J. T. Carlton, eds. *Light's Manual: Intertidal Invertebrates of the Central California Coast.* 3d ed. Berkeley and Los Angeles: University of California Press, 1975.

14.   Stephenson, T. A., and A. Stephenson. *Life between Tidemarks on Rocky Shores.* San Francisco: W. H. Freeman, 1972.

15.   Strathmann, M. F. *Reproduction and Development of Marine Invertebrates of the Northern Pacific Coast.* Seattle: University of Washington Press, 1987.

16.   Thomson, R. E. *Oceanography of the British Columbia Coast.* Canadian Special Publication of Fisheries and Aquatic Sciences 56. Ottawa: Department of Fisheries and Oceans, 1981.

17.   Waaland, J. R. *Common Seaweeds of the Pacific Coast.* Seattle: Pacific Search Press, 1977.

152

II

18.   Ayre, D. J., and R. K. Grosberg. Aggression, habituation, and clonal coexistence in the sea anemone *Anthopleura elegantissima. American Naturalist* 146 (1995): 427–453.

19.   Barnes, H., and E. S. Reese. Feeding in the pedunculate cirriped *Pollicipes polymerus* J. B. Sowerby. *Proceedings of the Zoological Society of London* 132 (1959): 569–585.

20. Barnes, H., and E. S. Reese. The behavior of the stalked intertidal barnacle *Pollicipes polymerus* J. B. Sowerby with special reference to its ecology and distribution. *Journal of Animal Ecology* 29 (1960): 169–185.

21. Birkeland, C. Biological observations on Cobb Seamount. *Northwest Science* 45, no. 3 (1971): 193–199.

22. Black, R. The effects of grazing by the limpet *Acmaea insessa* on the kelp *Egregia laevigata* in the intertidal zone. *Ecology* 57 (1976): 265–277.

23. Bloom, S. A. The motile escape response of a sessile prey: A sponge-scallop mutualism. *Journal of Experimental Marine Biology and Ecology* 17 (1975): 311–321.

24. Boekelheide, R. J., D. G. Ainley, S. H. Morrell, H. R. Huber, and T. J. Lewis. Common murre. In *Seabirds of the Farallon Islands,* ed. D. G. Ainley and R. J. Boekelheide, chap. 8. Stanford: Stanford University Press, 1990.

25. Bold, H. C., and M. J. Wynne. *Introduction to the Algae: Structure and Reproduction.* New Jersey: Prentice-Hall, 1978.

26. Bustamante, R. H., G. M. Branch, and S. Eekhout. Maintenance of an exceptional intertidal grazer biomass in South Africa: Subsidy by subtidal kelps. *Ecology* 76 (1995): 2314–2329.

27. Castenholz, R. W. The effect of grazing on marine littoral diatom populations. *Ecology* 42 (1961): 783–794.

28. Chadwick, E. M. P. A comparison of growth and abundance for tidal pool fishes in California and British Columbia. *Journal of Fish Biology* 8 (1976): 27–34.

29. Chia, F.-S. Brooding behavior of a six-rayed starfish, *Leptasterias hexactis. Biological Bulletin* 130 (1966): 304–315.

30. Connell, J. H. The influence of interspecific competition and other factors on the distribution of the barnacle *Chthamalus stellatus. Ecology* 42 (1961): 710–723.

31. Connell, J. H. A predator-prey system in the marine intertidal region. 1. *Balanus glandula* and several predatory species of *Thais. Ecological Monographs* 40 (1970): 49–78.

32. Connell, J. H. Community interactions on marine rocky intertidal shores. *Annual Review of Ecology and Systematics* 3 (1972): 169–192.

33. Cook, E. F. A study of food choices of two opistobranchs, *Rostanga pulchra* MacFarland and *Archidoris montereyensis* Cooperi. *Veliger* 4 (1962): 194–196.

34. Cott, H. B. *Adaptive Coloration in Animals.* London: Methuen, 1940.

35. Crisp, D. J. Factors influencing the settlement of marine invertebrate

larvae. In *Chemoreception in Marine Organisms,* ed. P. T. Grant and A. M. Mackee. London and New York: Academic Press, 1974.

36.   Culver, C. S., A. M. Kuris, and B. Beede. Identification and management of the exotic sabellid pest in California cultured abalone. California Sea Grant College System, Publication T-041. University of California, La Jolla, 1997.

37.   Dayton, P. K. Competition, disturbance, and community organization: The provision and subsequent utilization of space in a rocky intertidal community. *Ecological Monographs* 41 (1971): 351–389.

38.   Dayton, P. K. Two cases of resource partitioning in an intertidal community: Making the right prediction for the wrong reason. *American Naturalist* 107 (1973): 622–670.

39.   Dayton, P. K. Dispersion, dispersal, and persistence of the annual intertidal alga *Postelsia palmaeformis* Ruprecht. *Ecology* 54 (1973): 433–438.

40.   Denny, M. W., T. L. Daniel, and M. A. R. Koehl. Mechanical limits to size in wave-swept organisms. *Ecological Monographs* 55 (1984): 69–102.

41.   Dethier, M. N. Disturbance and recovery in intertidal pools: Maintenance of mosaic patterns. *Ecological Monographs* 54 (1984): 98–118.

42.   Druehl, L. D., and J. M. Green. Vertical distribution of intertidal seaweeds as related to patterns of submersion and emersion. *Marine Ecology Progress Series* 9 (1982): 163–170.

43.   Duggins, D. O. Kelp beds and sea otters: An experimental approach. *Ecology* 61 (1980): 447–453.

44.   Duggins, D. O. Sea urchins and kelp: The effects of short-term changes in urchin diet. *Limnology and Oceanography* 26 (1981): 391–394.

45.   Dunn, D. F. Reproduction of the externally brooding sea anemone *Epiactis prolifera* Verrill, 1869. *Biological Bulletin* 148 (1975): 199–218.

46.   Dunn, D. F. Dynamics of external brooding in the sea anemone *Epiactis prolifera. Marine Biology* 39 (1977): 41–47.

47.   Ebert, T. A. Growth rates of the sea urchin *Strongylocentrotus purpuratus* related to food availability and spine abrasion. *Ecology* 49 (1968): 1075–1091.

48.   Ebert, T. A. Recruitment in echinoderms. In *Echinoderm Studies,* ed. J. Lawrence and M. Jangoux. Rotterdam, Netherlands: Balkema, 1982.

49.   Edmunds, M. Protective mechanisms in the Eolidacea (Mollusca Nudibranchia). *Journal of the Linnean Society of London (Zoology)* 47 (1966): 27–71.

50.   Eppley, R. W., and C. R. Bovell. Sulphuric acid in *Desmarestia. Biological Bulletin* 115 (1958): 101–106.

51.   Estes, J. A., and D. O. Duggins. Sea otters and kelp forests in Alaska:

Generality and variation in a community ecology paradigm. *Ecological Monographs* 65 (1995): 75–100.

52. Estes, J. A., and J. F. Palmisano. Sea otters: Their role in structuring nearshore communities. *Science* 185 (1974): 1058–1060.

53. Estes, J. A., N. S. Smith, and J. F. Palmisano. Sea otter predation and community organization in the western Aleutian Islands, Alaska. *Ecology* 59 (1978): 822–833.

54. Estes, J. A., M. T. Tinker, T. M. Williams, and D. F. Doak. Killer whale predation on sea otters linking oceanic and nearshore ecosystems. *Science* 282 (1998): 473–476.

55. Feder, H. M. The food of the starfish *Pisaster ochraceus* along the California coast. *Ecology* 40 (1959): 721–724.

56. Feder, H. M. Growth and predation by the ochre sea star *Pisaster ochraceus* (Brandt) in Monterey Bay, California. *Ophelia* 8 (1970): 161–185.

57. Field, L. H. A description and experimental analysis of Batesian mimicry between a marine gastropod and an amphipod. *Pacific Science* 28 (1974): 439–447.

58. Forester, A. J. The association between the sponge *Halichondria panicea* (Pallas) and scallop *Chlamys yaria* (L.): A commensal-protective mutualism. *Journal of Experimental Marine Biology and Ecology* 36 (1979): 1–10.

59. Francis, L. Intraspecific aggression and its effect on the distribution of *Anthopleura elegantissima* and some related sea anemones. *Biological Bulletin* 144 (1973): 73–92.

60. Francis, L. Social organization within clones of the sea anemone *Anthopleura elegantissima*. *Biological Bulletin* 150 (1976): 361–376.

61. Frank, P. W. Effects of winter feeding on limpets by black oystercatchers, *Haematopus bachmani*. *Ecology* 63 (1982): 1352–1362.

62. Gaines, S. D. Herbivory and between-habitat diversity: The differential effectiveness of a plant defense. *Ecology* 66 (1985): 473–485.

63. Gerrodette, T. Dispersal of the solitary coral *Balanophyllia elegans* by demersal planular larvae. *Ecology* 62 (1981): 611–619.

64. Gosselin, L. A., and F.-S. Chia. Characterizing temperate rocky shores from the perspective of an early juvenile snail: The main threats to survival of newly hatched *Nucella emarginata*. *Marine Biology* 122 (1995): 625–635.

65. Harger, J. R. Competitive co-existence: Maintenance of interacting associations of the sea mussels *Mytilus edulis* and *Mytilus calfornianus*. *Veliger* 14 (1972): 387–410.

155

66. Hartwick, E. B. Foraging strategy of the black oystercatcher (*Haematopus bachmani* Audubon). *Canadian Journal of Zoology* 54 (1976): 142–155.

67. Hazlett, B. A. Interspecific negotiations: Mutual gain in exchanges of a limiting resource. *Animal Behavior* 31 (1983): 160–163.

68. Hedgpeth, J. W. The living edge. *Geoscience and Man* 14 (1976): 17.

69. Hines, A. H. Reproduction in three species of intertidal barnacles from central California. *Biological Bulletin* 154 (1978): 262–281.

70. Hines, A. H., and J. H. Pearse. Abalones, shells, and sea otters: Dynamics of prey populations in central California. *Ecology* 63 (1982): 547–560.

71. Jackson, J. B. C., and L. Buss. Allelopathy and spatial competition among coral reef invertebrates. *Proceedings of the National Academy of Science (USA)* 72 (1975): 5160–5163.

72. Jensen, G. C. *Pacific Coast Crabs and Shrimp.* Monterey, CA: Sea Challengers, 1995.

73. Koehl, M. A. R. The interaction of moving water and sessile organisms. *Scientific American* (1982) 247:124–134.

74. Koehl, M. A. R., and S. A. Wainwright. Mechanical adaptations of a giant kelp. *Limnology and Oceanography* 22 (1977): 1067–1071.

75. Kvitek, R. G., A. R. DeGange, and M. K. Beitler. Paralytic shellfish poisoning toxins mediate feeding behavior of sea otters. *Limnology and Oceanography* 36 (1991): 393–404.

76. Landenberger, D. E. Studies on selective feeding in the Pacific starfish *Pisaster* in southern California. *Ecology* 49 (1968): 1062–1075.

77. Lang, J. C. Interspecific aggression by scleractinian corals. II. Why the race is not only to the swift. *Bulletin of Marine Science* 23 (1973): 260–279.

78. Lindberg, D. R. *Acmaeidae: Gastropoda, Mollusca.* Pacific Grove, CA: Boxwood Press, 1981.

79. Lubchenco, J. Plant species diversity in a marine intertidal community: Importance of herbivore food preference and algal competitive abilities. *American Naturalist* 112 (1978): 23–39.

80. Lubchenco, J., and J. Cubit. Heteromorphic life histories of certain algae as adaptations to variations in herbivory. *Ecology* 61 (1980): 676–687.

81. Lubchenco, J., and S. D. Gaines. A unified approach to marine plant herbivore interactions. I. Populations and communities. *Annual Review of Ecology and Systematics* 12 (1981): 405–437.

82. Mann, K. H. Seaweeds: Their productivity and strategy for growth. *Science* 182 (1973): 975–981.

156

83.   Margolin, A. S. The mantle response of *Diodora aspera. Animal Behavior* 12 (1964): 187–194.

84.   Margolin, A. S. A running response of *Acmaea* to seastars. *Ecology* 45 (1964): 191–193.

85.   Mauzey, K. P. Feeding behavior and reproductive cycles in *Pisaster ochraceus. Biological Bulletin* 131 (1966): 127–144.

86.   Mauzey, K. P., C. Birkeland, and P. K. Dayton. Feeding behavior of asteroids and escape responses of their prey in the Puget Sound region. *Ecology* 49 (1968): 603–619.

87.   McDonald, G. R. *Guide to the Nudibranchs of California*. Melbourne, FL: American Malacologists, Inc. 1980.

88.   Menge, B. A. Foraging strategy of a starfish in relation to actual prey availability and environmental predictability. *Ecological Monographs* 42 (1972): 25–50.

89.   Menge, B. A. Effect of wave action and competition on brooding and reproductive effort in the seastar *Leptasterias hexactis. Ecology* 55 (1974): 84–93.

90.   Menge, B. A. Brood or broadcast? The adaptive significance of different reproductive strategies in the two intertidal sea stars *Leptasterias hexactis* and *Pisaster ochraceus. Marine Biology* 31 (1975): 87–100.

91.   Miller, B. A., and R. B. Emlet. Influence of nearshore hydrodynamics on larval abundance and settlement of sea urchins *Strongylocentrotus franciscanus* and *S. purpuratus* in the Oregon upwelling zone. *Marine Ecology Progress Series* 148 (1997): 83–94.

92.   Muscatine, L. Experiments on green algae coexistent with zooxanthellae in sea anemones. *Pacific Science* 25 (1971): 13–21.

93.   Navarrete, S. A. Variable predation: Effects of whelks on a mid-intertidal successional community. *Ecological Monographs* 66 (1996): 301–321.

94.   Nicol, E. A. T. The feeding mechanism, formation of the tube, and physiology of digestion in *Sabella pavonina. Transactions of the Royal Society, Edinburgh* 56 (1930): 537–596.

95.   Nicotri, M. E. Grazing effects of four marine intertidal herbivores on the microflora. *Ecology* 58 (1977): 1020–1032.

96.   Osman, R. W., and J. A. Haugness. Mutualism among sessile invertebrates: A mediator of competition and predation. *Science* 211 (1981): 846–848.

97.   Ostarello, G. L. Natural history of the hydrocoral *Allopora californica* Verill (1866). *Biological Bulletin* 145 (1973): 548–564.

157

98. Paine, R. T. Food web complexity and species diversity. *American Naturalist* 100 (1966): 65–70.

99. Paine, R. T. A note on trophic complexity and species diversity. *American Naturalist* 103 (1969): 91–93.

100. Paine, R. T. Intertidal community structure: Experimental studies on the relationship between a dominant competitor and its principal predator. *Oecologia* 15 (1974): 93–120.

101. Paine, R. T. Disaster, catastrophe, and local persistence of the sea palm *Postelsia palmaeformis. Science* 205 (1979): 685–687.

102. Paine, R. T. Food webs: Linkage, interaction strength, and community infrastructure. *Journal of Animal Ecology* 49 (1980): 667–685.

103. Paine, R. T. Ecological determinism in the competition for space. *Ecology* 65 (1984): 1339–1348.

104. Paine, R. T. Marine rocky shores and community ecology: An experimentalist's perspective. In *Excellence in Ecology,* no. 4, ed. O. Kinne. Oldendorf, Germany: Ecology Institute, 1994.

105. Paine, R. T., and S. A. Levin. Intertidal landscapes: Disturbance and the dynamics of pattern. *Ecological Monographs* 51 (1981): 145–178.

106. Paine, R. T., C. J. Slocum, and D. O. Duggins. Growth and longevity in the crustose red alga *Petrocelis middendorffii. Marine Biology* 51 (1979): 185–192.

107. Paine, R. T., and T. H. Suchanek. Convergence of ecological processes between independently evolved competitive dominants: A tunicate-mussel comparison. *Evolution* 37 (1983): 821–831.

108. Paine, R. T., and R. L. Vadas. The effects of grazing by sea urchins, *Strongylocentrotus* sp., on benthic algal populations. *Limnology and Oceanography* 14 (1969): 710–719.

109. Palmer, A. R. Prey selection by thaidid gastropods: Some observational and experimental field tests of foraging models. *Oecologia* 62 (1984): 162–172.

110. Palumbi, S. R. How body plans limit acclimation: Responses of a demosponge to wave force. *Ecology* 67 (1986): 208–214.

111. Parrish, J. K., and P. D. Boersma. Muddy waters. *American Scientist* 83 (1995): 112–115.

112. Pernet, B. Development of the keyhole and growth rate in *Diodora aspera* (Gastropoda: Fissurellidae). *Veliger* 40 (1997): 77–83.

113. Pfister, C. A. Estimating competition coefficients from census data: A test with field manipulations of tidepool fishes. *American Naturalist* 146 (1995): 271–291.

114. Quinn, J. F. Competitive hierarchies in marine benthic communities. *Oecologia* 54 (1982): 129–135.

115. Rigg, G. B., and R. C. Miller. Intertidal plant and animal zonation in the vicinity of Neah Bay, Washington. *Proceedings of the California Academy of Science* 26 (1949): 323–351.

116. Rivest, B. R. Development and the influence of nurse egg allotment on hatching size in *Searlesia dira* (Reeve, 1846) (Prosobranchia: Buccinidae). *Journal of Experimental Marine Biology and Ecology* 69 (1983): 217–241.

117. Roden, G. I. On statistical estimation of monthly extreme sea-surface temperature along the west coast of the United States. *Journal of Marine Research* 21 (1963): 172–190.

118. Russ, G. R. Overgrowth in a marine epifaunal community: Competitive hierarchies and competitive networks. *Oecologia* 53 (1982): 12–19.

119. Scagel, R. F. *An Investigation on Marine Plants near Hardy Bay.* Vol. 1. Victoria, B.C.: Provincial Department of Fisheries, 1947.

120. Scheltema, R. The dispersal of the larvae of shoal-water benthic invertebrate species over long distances by ocean currents. In *European Marine Biology Symposium,* vol. 4, ed. D. J. Crisp. New York: Cambridge University Press, 1971.

121. Schroeter, S. C., J. Dixon, and J. Kastendiek. Effects of the starfish *Patiria miniata* on the distribution of the sea urchin *Lytechinus anamesus* in a southern Californian kelp forest. *Oecologia* 56 (1983): 141–147.

122. Sebens, K. P. Recruitment and habitat selection in the intertidal sea anemones *Anthopleura elegantissima* (Brandt) and *A. xanthogrammica* (Brandt). *Journal of Experimental Marine Biology and Ecology* 59 (1982): 103–124.

123. Sebens, K. P. The limits to indeterminate growth: An optimal size model applied to passive suspension feeders. *Ecology* 63 (1982): 209–222.

124. Sebens, K. P. Population dynamics and habitat suitability of the intertidal sea anemones *Anthopleura elegantissima* and *A. xanthogrammica*. *Ecological Monographs* 53 (1983): 405–433.

125. Seed, R., and T. H. Suchanek. Population and community ecology of *Mytilus*. In *The Mussel Mytilus: Ecology, Physiology, Genetics, and Culture,* ed. E. M. Gosling, 87–169. Amsterdam: Elsevier Science, 1992.

126. Slocum, C. J. Differential susceptibility to grazers in two phases of an intertidal alga: Advantages of heteromorphic generations. *Journal of Experimental Marine Biology and Ecology* 46 (1980): 99–110.

127. Sousa, W. P. Disturbance in marine intertidal boulder fields: The nonequilibrium maintenance of species diversity. *Ecology* 60 (1979): 1225–1239.

128. Sousa, W. P. Intertidal mosaics: Patch size, propagule availability, and spatially variable patterns of succession. *Ecology* 65 (1984): 1918–1935.

129. Spight, T. M. Hatching size and the distribution of nurse eggs among prosobranch embryos. *Biological Bulletin* 150 (1976): 491–499.

130. Steneck, R. S. A limpet-coralline alga association: Adaptations and defenses between a selective herbivore and its prey. *Ecology* 63 (1982): 502–522.

131. Steneck, R. S. Escalating herbivory and resulting adaptive trends in calcareous algal crusts. *Paleobiology* 9 (1983): 44–61.

132. Steneck, R. S., and R. T. Paine. Ecological and taxonomic studies of shallow-water encrusting Corallinaceae (Phodophyta) of the boreal northeastern Pacific. *Phycologia* 25 (1986): 221–240.

133. Strathmann, R. R. The spread of sibling larvae of sedentary marine invertebrates. *American Naturalist* 108, no. 959 (1974): 29–44.

134. Strathmann, R. R., E. S. Branscomb, and K. Vedder. Fatal errors in set as a cost of dispersal and the influence of intertidal flora on set of barnacles. *Oecologia* 48 (1981): 13–18.

135. Suchanek, T. H. The role of disturbance in the evolution of life history strategies in the intertidal mussels *Mytilus edulis* and *Mytilus californianus*. *Oecologia* 50 (1981): 143–152.

136. Tegner, M. J., and P. K. Dayton. Sea urchin recruitment patterns and implications of commercial fishing. *Science* 196 (1977): 324–326.

137. Trapp, J. L. Variations in summer diet of glaucous-winged gulls in the western Aleutian Islands: An ecological interpretation. *Wilson Bulletin* 91 (1979): 412–419.

138. Turner, T. Facilitation as a successional mechanism in a rocky intertidal community. *American Naturalist* 121 (1983): 729–738.

139. Vadas, R. L. Preferential feeding: An optimization strategy in sea urchins. *Ecological Monographs* 47 (1977): 337–371.

140. Vance, R. R. Competition and mechanism of coexistence in three sympatric species of intertidal hermit crabs. *Ecology* 53 (1972): 1062–1074.

141. Vance, R. R. The role of shell adequacy in behavioral interactions involving hermit crabs. *Ecology* 53 (1972): 1075–1083.

142. Wagner, R. H., D. W. Phillips, J. D. Standing, and C. Hand. Commensalism or mutualism: Attraction of a sea star towards its symbiotic polychaete. *Journal of Experimental Marine Biology and Ecology* 39 (1979): 205–210.

143. West, L. Interindividual variation in prey selection by the snail *Nucella* (= Thais) *emarginata*. *Ecology* 67 (1986): 798–809.

144. Wethey, D. S. Effects of crowding on fecundity in barnacles: *Semibalanus*

(Balanus) balanoides, Balanus glandula, and Chthamalus dalli. Canadian Journal of Zoology 62 (1984): 1788–1795.

145. Wethey, D. S. Spatial pattern in barnacle settlement: Day-to-day changes during the settlement season. Journal of Marine Biological Association of the U.K. 64 (1984): 687–698.

146. Wootton, J. T. The nature and consequences of indirect effects in ecological communities. Annual Review of Ecology and Systematics 25 (1994): 443–466.

147. Wootton, J. T. Predicting direct and indirect effects: An integrated approach using experiments and path analysis. Ecology 75 (1994): 151–165.

III

Plate no.	Reference no.	Plate no.	Reference no.	Plate no.	Reference no.
1	8, 12, 14, 16, 68, 110	31	77, 104, 114, 118	54	9
2	4	32	71, 118	55	50
3	4	33	39, 101	56	50
4	8, 107	34	94, 96	57	83, 84, 112
5	37	36	23, 58, 96	58	44
6	12, 14, 42	39	61, 66, 137, 147	59	80, 106, 126
10	1, 3, 6, 9, 10, 13	40	79, 81	60	80, 106, 126
11	82	41	22, 27, 37, 95	61	74, 119
12	40, 73	43	44, 47, 108, 131, 136	62	26
13	30, 32, 37, 103	44	139	63	130, 132
14	55, 56, 85, 86, 88	45	78, 130, 132	64	41, 138
17	40, 100	46	121	65	15
18	77	47	4, 31, 37, 93, 109, 143	66	21, 45, 46
19	37, 98	48	4, 31, 37, 93, 109, 143	67	15, 29, 64, 89, 116, 129
20	18, 59, 60	49	55, 56, 76, 85, 98, 102	68	15, 29, 64, 89, 116, 129
21	18, 59, 60	50	11, 28, 34, 113	69	18, 59, 60, 122
22	97	51	38, 122, 124	70	18, 59, 60, 122
24	67, 140, 141	52	73, 94, 123	71	15, 87
25	107, 125	53	87, 96, 142, 146	72	15, 87
27	30, 32, 37, 144			73	15, 87
28	65, 98, 104, 107			75	90
30	19, 20			76	120, 133

Plate no.	Reference no.	Plate no.	Reference no.	Plate no.	Reference no.
77	35, 69, 134, 144, 145	93	33	107	97
		94	34, 88	108	97
78	48, 91, 136	97	11, 34, 113	110	37, 105, 127, 135
79	86	98	11, 34, 113	111	37, 105, 127, 135
81	62	99	72	112	108
83	25	100	63	113	43, 44, 51, 52, 53, 54, 70, 75, 99
84	50	101	92		
85	17, 128	102	86		
88	58, 110	103	20	114	121
89	49, 87	104	42, 68, 115	115	36
90	4	105	39, 101	116	24
92	57	106	39, 101	117	111

162

Photograph Locations and Dates

Plate 1	Tatoosh Island, Washington	June 1982
2	Tatoosh Island, Washington	June 1982
3	Tatoosh Island, Washington	June 1998
4	Tatoosh Island, Washington	May 1982
5	Tatoosh Island, Washington	Aug. 1984
6	Tatoosh Island, Washington	May 1982
7	Tatoosh Island, Washington	June 1979
8	Tatoosh Island, Washington	June 1984
9	Tatoosh Island, Washington	July 1983
10	Tatoosh Island, Washington	June 1979
11	Tatoosh Island, Washington	May 1980
12	Tatoosh Island, Washington	June 1979
13	Point Reyes, California	Jan. 2000
14	Duk Point, Washington	Feb. 1980
15	Tatoosh Island, Washington	May 1983
16	Tatoosh Island, Washington	July 1982
17	Tatoosh Island, Washington	June 1984
18	Tatoosh Island, Washington	April 1980
19	Torch Bay, Alaska	July 1981
20	Tatoosh Island, Washington	May 1983
21	Point Reyes, California	May 1983
22	Tatoosh Island, Washington	Sept. 1979

23	Torch Bay, Alaska	July 1981
24	Tatoosh Island, Washington	May 1983
25	Tatoosh Island, Washington	May 1982
26	Tatoosh Island, Washington	June 1982
27	Tatoosh Island, Washington	Sept. 1979
28	Tatoosh Island, Washington	Aug. 1982
29	Tatoosh Island, Washington	June 1980
30	Tatoosh Island, Washington	June 1981
31	Torch Bay, Alaska	July 1980
32	Torch Bay, Alaska	Aug. 1981
33	Tatoosh Island, Washington	June 1982
34	Tatoosh Island, Washington	July 1983
35	Tatoosh Island, Washington	July 1980
36	Tatoosh Island, Washington	June 1981
37	Salt Point, California	July 1976
38	Tatoosh Island, Washington	April 1983
39	Tatoosh Island, Washington	July 1981
40	Waadah Island, Washington	May 1980
41	Salt Point, California	May 1975
42	Waadah Island, Washington	May 1978
43	Tatoosh Island, Washington	June 1981
44	Tatoosh Island, Washington	June 1981
45	Tatoosh Island, Washington	Aug. 1982
46	Point Reyes, California	March 2000
47	Torch Bay, Alaska	June 1981
48	Torch Bay, Alaska	June 1981
49	Tatoosh Island, Washington	June 1982
50	Tatoosh Island, Washington	June 1980
51	Tatoosh Island, Washington	July 1981
52	Tatoosh Island, Washington	April 1984
53	Tatoosh Island, Washington	March 1980
54	Point Reyes, California	May 2000
55	Tatoosh Island, Washington	June 1982
56	Tatoosh Island, Washington	June 1982
57	Tatoosh Island, Washington	June 1982
58	Seal Rock, Washington	May 1981
59	Portage Head, Washington	June 1981
60	Portage Head, Washington	June 1981

61	Tatoosh Island, Washington	Aug. 1984
62	Tatoosh Island, Washington	Feb. 1984
63	Tatoosh Island, Washington	July 1980
64	Tatoosh Island, Washington	Aug. 1982
65	Tatoosh Island, Washington	May 1982
66	Tatoosh Island, Washington	April 1984
67	Botanical Beach, Vancouver Island, British Columbia	July 1979
68	Tatoosh Island, Washington	June 1982
69	Tatoosh Island, Washington	Aug. 1982
70	Tatoosh Island, Washington	Aug. 1979
71	Tatoosh Island, Washington	June 1981
72	Torch Bay, Alaska	July 1980
73	Tatoosh Island, Washington	July 1981
74	Tatoosh Island, Washington	July 1983
75	Tatoosh Island, Washington	July 1983
76	Pile Point, San Juan Island, Washington	April 1979
77	Torch Bay, Alaska	Aug. 1983
78	Tatoosh Island, Washington	May 1981
79	Tatoosh Island, Washington	Aug. 1984
80	Tatoosh Island, Washington	July 1983
81	Point Reyes, California	May 1975
82	Torch Bay, Alaska	Aug. 1981
83	Botanical Beach, Vancouver Island, British Columbia	July 1979
84	Tatoosh Island, Washington	May 1984
85	Point Reyes, California	July 1975
86	Tatoosh Island, Washington	Aug. 1984
87	Point Reyes, California	June 1975
88	Tatoosh Island, Washington	July 1981
89	Tatoosh Island, Washington	May 1983
90	Point Reyes, California	June 2000
91	Moss Beach, California	June 1976
92	Tatoosh Island, Washington	June 1979
93	Tatoosh Island, Washington	July 1983
94	Point Reyes, California	Feb. 1999
95	Torch Bay, Alaska	July 1981

96	Tatoosh Island, Washington	May 1984
97	Tatoosh Island, Washington	July 1979
98	Point Reyes, California	Aug. 1976
99	Tatoosh Island, Washington	June 1982
100	Tatoosh Island, Washington	June 1980
101	Tatoosh Island, Washington	June 1980
102	Tatoosh Island, Washington	May 1980
103	Tatoosh Island, Washington	July 1980
104	Seal Rock, Washington	June 1981
105	Tatoosh Island, Washington	July 1983
106	Tatoosh Island, Washington	June 1998
107	Tatoosh Island, Washington	June 1980
108	Tatoosh Island, Washington	July 1981
109	Tatoosh Island, Washington	April 1983
110	Tatoosh Island, Washington	Feb. 1981
111	Tatoosh Island, Washington	June 1983
112	Moss Beach, California	June 1976
113	Monterey Bay, California	March 1993
114	Point Reyes, California	May 1999
115	Bodega Marine Lab, California	March 1999
116	Tatoosh Island, Washington	July 1979
117	Tatoosh Island, Washington	April 1983
118	Moss Beach, California	June 1998
119	Tatoosh Island, Washington	May 1982

168

170

Microcladia sp. (algae), 14
Mimicry, 92, 104
 limpet shell pattern, 114
Mobile organisms
 predation by, 23, 58
 space competition by, 23,
  32, 34
Murre, 136
Mussel, 23, 124
 dominance in intertidal
  communities, 36, 45
 feeding behavior, 60
 harvesting of, 144
 kelp shredded by, 36
 mobility, 36
 sea palm overgrowth,
  38
 shell thickness, 46
 space competition with
  barnacles, 36
 vulnerability to wave
  action, 6, 36, 128
 *See also scientific names
  of specific mussels*
Mussel beds, 32, 36
 damage from walking on,
  143–44
 disruption from harvest-
  ing, 144
 gaps in, 118, 130
 habitat characteristics, 36
 patch sizes, 130
 sea anemones in, 56
 wave action and, 6, 36,
  128
Mycale sp. (yellow sponge),
 126
Mytilus californianus (California mussel), 24, 122
 classification of, 3
 dominance in Pacific
  coast intertidal
  communities, 36
 gaps in beds, 130
 as starfish prey, 56
Mytilus edulis. See *Mytilus
 trossulus*
Mytilus trossulus (blue
 mussel), 122
 as whelk prey, 54

Natural selection, 66
 breeding aggregations, 88
 clutch sizes and, 66
 dispersal phenomenon,
  67–68
 larval stage duration and,
  86
 reproductive strategies,
  66–67, 69
 See also Reproduction
Nearshore habitat, significance of, 16
Nereocystis (kelp), 48
 six-armed starfish and, 76
Nereocystis luetkeana (bull
 kelp)
 beached, as food and
  habitat, 72
 life cycle, 72
 reproduction, 72
Notoacmaea scutum (limpet),
 green algae on, 40
Nucella (snail), direct
 development, 67
Nucella canaliculata (snail)
 egg capsules, 78
 predation by, 54
 reproduction, 78
Nudibranch
 amphipod attacks on, 60
 color, 102
 diet, 102, 104
 egg ribbons, 82
 reproduction, 82

Octopus, ability to change
 color, 108
Oedignathus sp. (crab), as
 sea anemone prey, 58
Oil spills, 120, 136
Oligocottus maculosus
 (sculpin), cryptic
 coloration, 108
Ophiopholus aculelata
 (brittle starfish), 32
 coloration, 100
Ophlitaspongia sp. (red
 sponge), 126
Ophlitaspongia pennata (red
 sponge)

as nudibranch prey, 104
 pigments incorporated by
  nudibranchs, 104
Oregonia gracilis (spider
 crab)
 camouflage by other
  organisms, 110
 cryptic coloration, 110
Orthasterias koehleri
 (starfish), 112
Otter. *See* Sea otter
Overgrowth relationships,
 18, 33, 40
 morphological adapta-
  tions, 40
Overharvesting, 118–19, 138
Oyster, 119
Oystercatcher, prey species
 for, 46

Pacific coast (North
 America), 1–2, 4
 Atlantic coast compared
  to, 4
 habitat richness of, 1
 laws on harvesting and
  collecting marine
  organisms, 144
 predator-prey interac-
  tions, 44
 shellfish farming
  industry, 134
 tides, 4, 141–42
Pagurus (hermit crab), color
 discrimination by, 90
Pagurus samuelis (hermit
 crab), in *Tegula* shell, 32
Patiria miniata. See *Asterina
 miniata*
Pelvetia fastigiata (brown
 alga), color, 98
Periwinkle
 algae as prey, 48
 communal feeding, 48
 grazing trails, 48
Petrocelis middendorffii (red
 alga life phase), 70
Phidiana crassicornis
 (nudibranch)
 cannibalism, 82

171

173

Tonicella lineata (lined
  chiton)
  color, modified by diet,
    108
  grazing on coralline
    algae, 52
  markings, 108
Tunicates, 14, 122
  interspecific space
    competition, 26

Ulva sp. (green alga), 14, 94
  in mussel bed gap, 130
Unwanted species, 20, 119,
    138
  carnivorous gastropods,
    119
  from grocery stores and
    aquariums, 145
  sabellid polychaete (fan
    worm), 134–35
  from ships, 119, 145

See also Introduced
  species
Uria aalge (murre), 136
  oil-spill coating effects,
    136
Urticina sp. (sea anemone),
  98

Velella velella (by-the-wind
  sailor), as prey, 64
Vision
  color, 90–91
  underwater, 90

Washington, 4, 10, 46
  See also Pacific coast
Water pollution. *See*
  Pollution
Wave action, 138
  habitat richness and, 6, 42
  intertidal zone bound-
    aries and, 6, 122

mussel vulnerability to, 6,
    36, 126
Whelks, prey species for, 54

Zonation (of intertidal
    organisms), 122
  assessment, experimental
    methods, 16–18
  boundary delineations, 6,
    10, 122
  constancy of, 10, 121,
    122
  disturbances, 121
  governing factors, 2
  predation patterns and,
    18
  tidal influence on, 10
  wave-exposed habitats,
    122
Zostera (sea grass), 74
  as nursery for fish and
    crustaceans, 74

174

Designer:	Steve Renick
Compositor:	Integrated Composition Systems
Text:	11/16 Scala
Display:	Scala Sans
Printer/Binder:	Global Fibers
Indexer:	Beaver Wood Associates